W. P. Balfern

Lessons from Jesus: Or the Zeachings of Divine Love

W. P. Balfern

Lessons from Jesus: Or the Zeachings of Divine Love

ISBN/EAN: 9783337166045

Printed in Europe, USA, Canada, Australia, Japan

Cover: Foto ©Lupo / pixelio.de

More available books at **www.hansebooks.com**

LESSONS FROM JESUS:

OR,

THE TEACHINGS OF DIVINE LOVE.

By W. P. BALFERN,

AUTHOR OF "GLIMPSES OF JESUS."

&

"And all thy children shall be taught of the LORD; and great shall be the
peace of thy children."—ISA. liv. 13.

NEW YORK:
SHELDON & COMPANY.

BOSTON: GOULD & LINCOLN.

1859.

PREFACE.

It is considered very wrong by many, to publish a book which travels over a path marked by the footprints of the illustrious dead; and by others, unless a work is possessed of so much power and originality that it is likely to stand side by side, in fraternal juxtaposition, with the intellectual and spiritual treasures destined to live so long as this world's literature shall last, it is thought to be a crime to publish. In these sentiments the writer does not share; for however industriously the greatest may have laboured in the field of truth, their inferiors who follow them will frequently find some few ears which it may be useful to gather up; or, to change the figure, it may be their work to give another setting to the thoughts of those who have departed, more adapted to the wants of the age in which they live. In this way, too, through inferior men, the mighty dead reproduce themselves, and exert an undying influence; and the sweet and instructive voices of the past, that would long have been hushed in silence, are heard through the writings and utterances of living men, ringing forth an everlasting chime amid the discords and changes ever attendant upon the growth of intellect and the march of mind.

The object of the writer is to gain for the *whole* Gospel a more extensive and affectionate reception among those who may have apprehended it but partially, and to bring out its adaptation to the varied experiences both of the old and the young, the decided and the undecided, the believer and the sceptic :—subsidiary to these designs, also to raise a note of warning, as to the designs of many, who either openly or covertly are seeking to rob the Church of those *doctrines* which have been, and must continue to be, the only source of her spiritual strength, beauty, and usefulness, while travelling through this wilderness of time.

The reader will perceive that some of the most beautiful poems in this work, are selected from a series entitled " Lyra Germanica." Should the liberty taken in extracting them be the means of leading any to purchase the volumes themselves, it will afford great pleasure to the writer of this book, as he is acquainted with no poetry more fully equal to its high and holy aim, or better adapted to strengthen and feed a devotional spirit.

CONTENTS.

LESSONS FROM JESUS;

OR,

THE TEACHINGS OF DIVINE LOVE.

"At Thy through-pierced feet,
I'll humbly take my seat;
　　There's heaven's enjoyment:
To give Thee thanks and praise
For all Thy love and grace
　　Be my employment."

Oh! may we here in faith abide
At Jesus' feet, whate'er betide;
May neither sin nor change remove
Our hearts from resting in His love!

LESSONS FROM JESUS.

Mary at the Feet of Jesus;

OR,

THE MODEL DISCIPLE.

" Who also sat at Jesus' feet."—Luke x. 39.

OF the author of the "Divina Commedia," a certain celebrated writer has said, "I think that the central man of all the world, as representing in *perfect balance* the imaginative, moral, and intellectual faculties, all at their highest, is Dante." How much more sublimely true is this of HIM who while He was really man with us was no less God; whose mind was a perfect mirror of God's law from the cradle to the tomb; and who, indeed, embodied in Himself all perfection both human and divine. Of the great poet thus eloquently eulogised, we are sure, that, though the powers of his mind, like a majestic harp, gave forth sweet and illustrious music, yet there *were* the discordant notes incident to humanity; and the wonderful singer himself, in his latter days wrote, "I have already written many times regarding love in the sweetest, most beautiful, and graceful rhymes I was able, and I exerted all my powers to refine them. They no longer satisfy my desires, for I know that I have *vainly expended my labours*, and been ill repaid. I now withdraw my hand from writing any longer on this *false love*, but will discourse on God as befits a Christian." Of this false love he thus wrote:—

"A slave before, Thou hast released me. Thou,
   By every art and mode that could be tried,
Did'st win the freedom that I cherish now.
   Continue Thy beneficence to me,
So that my soul, which Thou hast purified,
   May lose its mortal bonds, approved by Thee."

How beautifully consistent and congruous would this language be as applied to Him whose love is the source of heaven's purity and joy, and whose words proclaim liberty to the captive and the opening of the prison to those who are bound. Of One whom we can truly say,

"That, day by day,
Like one who never can be truly known,
   His beauty grows ;"

and who, to the sanctified heart, must ever be "the chiefest among ten thousand and the altogether lovely." Strange that the lips of genius have so little to say about Him! The vast powers of Dante, and many other kindred minds, excite our wonder, and there are many other things in the world that perpetually call it forth. Our own physical and moral constitution, the flowers beneath our feet, and the stars above our heads—every object, indeed, which surrounds us, whether great or small, presents to the contemplative mind elements of thought and astonishment. Still there is nothing in this visible universe, with all its multitudinous objects, harmonies, and adaptations, which excites so much sublime and intelligent wonder in the mind of a Christian, as the incarnation of the Son of God.

> Here reason pales her wonted fires,
> And mute with holy awe adores.

That He, who was God over all, should so identify Himself with us as to become bone of our bone and flesh of our flesh,—should so veil the brightness of His face that sinful creatures could gaze upon it and live,—that He should come so near to us, as that we could reach Him, yea, even sit at His feet,—that He should wear our nature, use our words, and through them pour His great and loving thoughts into our hearts, is wonderful indeed.

"How beautiful upon the mountains are the feet of those who bring glad tidings!" said one of

old.   How beautiful do the servants of Christ appear, as, constrained by faith and love, they stand
forth to make known to dying men the glories of
their Lord!   How 'much more beautiful does He
appear, whose glorious deeds furnish them with
the glad tidings they proclaim; who robed Himself in frailty, and came over the huge mountains
of our guilt, and through seas of suffering and
sorrow, to reach and to save us!   Well may we,
indeed, sit at His feet who came to guide us to·
paths of purity and peace.   Reader, who is thy
teacher? with what school or sect dost thou stand
identified?   We wish to direct thy attention to a'
pleasing and instructive scene—a woman sitting
at the feet of Jesus.   It was a lowly place, but it
became her well, and in the temple of truth she
lives illustrious, a fair example to all, and thus
she shall appear to ages yet unborn.

At whose feet did she sit?   At the feet of
Jesus.   And who was He?   Isaiah gives His
name in full: "His name shall be called Wonderful, Counsellor, the Mighty God, the Everlasting Father, the Prince of peace."   Wise was this
woman's choice: she stooped to take the highest
place; well might the angels envy her.   Who
shall be great if she is not; so near the King of
kings *she sat*, on terms of intimacy with the Lord
of all: this might be doubted, but it was even so,
such was the condescension of our God.   What
can we say?   The reader may test this fact—it

is not impossible even now to sit at Jesus's feet.
Dost thou inquire how?—by thinking over His
words in faith and prayer. Christ is not far from
any one of us, and to the humble, waiting spirit,
will make known His love, though now enthroned
above. We may be intimate with God; although
so great, He calls us to His feet, He claims our
ear: " Hearken" (He says), " O daughter, and
consider and incline thine ear; forget also thine
own people and thy father's house: so shall the
King greatly desire thy beauty; for He is my
Lord, and worship thou Him." It is not His will
that we should wander through the universe like
orphans, uncertain, neglected, sad. There is a
place where He unveils His love, reveals His
face—a father's heart—and speaks in language we
can understand; where His great mind spreads
out its ample stores to satisfy the longing soul.
The feet of Jesus is this place : reader, hast thou
been there? Thou hast climbed the summit of
some lofty mountain, it may be with toil and
pain, to gaze upon the outspread charms of Nature's face: more at the feet of Jesus thou mayest
see, without the toil and weariness.

Hast thou not looked into His face? Thou
hast not seen much; thou hast not seen the mirror of His love who made thee, His wisdom,
beauty, grace. Look up from thence, and thou
wilt see more than the stars; the world a *little
thing*, and truths we all should know, but which

on Nature's brow, however fair, we never should read.

She sat at Jesus's feet. O how humility ex-alted her: it raised her to the bosom of her Lord, brought commendation from the lips of God! She meekly stooped to bear His mild and easy yoke,—too glad to receive instruction from His lips. She *sat*—she stayed, awhile, she waited on His words. With open heart, like Lydia's, she listened anxious to learn, and held. her memory, like a golden vase, to catch each precious fragrant drop of truth which came distilling from His lips. Many rush into the presence of Christ with steeled hearts, and ears half closed, attention fast asleep, and reason's eye filmed o'er by prejudice, and rush away again, and wonder they are not wise. Reader, if thou wouldst know the Lord, stay with Him for a time; ponder His words, until their *meaning* makes them sweet to thee; hide thou the precious grain within, and give it time to fructify; upon the walls of the dark chamber of vain ima-gery within, let the words of Jesus shine like stars, and gaze upon them until their light beams cheerfully upon thee, and brings to thee intelli-gence of things this godless, idle, thoughtless world sees not, of joys, and peace, and rest, and which lie far away beyond the reach of all its noise, its teaching, and its praise.

"Who also sat at Jesus's feet." *How comely her position.* Was it not right to bow to Him

who stooped from heaven to suffering and death
that He might lift her to a throne? Comely—
how beautiful to see the creature's mind accord
with God's, to mark a soul stooping to slake its
thirst at life's own fountain! How wise for frailty
to repose on everlasting strength; for conscious
ignorance to hang upon the lips which never err;
a spotted soul to hide beneath His priestly vest,
who never sinned.

How great its advantages. It is here the whispers of a Saviour's love are heard, the voice of
wisdom too often lost amid the din of life; and
here His face is seen whose unveiled charms fill
heaven with bliss; here peace resides, and fills
the quiet heart with overflowing joy. And when
the universe shall reel, and nations wail responsive
to the archangel's blast, the meek disciple at the
feet of Christ shall lift his smiling face and say,
" My Saviour reigns." Reader, it is possible by
faith and prayer to sit at the feet of Jesus now;
but self and pride must fall, the world must be
forsaken.

Art thou prepared for this?

Remember that he who will not sit at the
feet of Jesus now, must come *beneath* His feet at
last.

A place there is where friends can meet,
  Though death remove and seas divide;
'Tis found in Christ, 'tis at His feet,
  Hard by His cross and wounded side.

Here, freed from care, the poor rejoice,
   Forget their toils and lose their grief;
The waiting heart hears mercy's voice,
   And finds the balm which brings relief.

Here faith and love together dwell,
   With weeping eyes here oft adore,
Record His triumph over hell,
   Who all their sins and sorrows bore.

Here peace with outspread wings abides,
   And folds her children to her breast,
And, while the scoffing world derides,
   Dries up their tears and gives them rest

"Alas, for man who hath no sense
Of gratefulness or confidence,
  But still rejects and raves ;
That all God's love can hardly win
One soul from taking pride in sin,
  And pleasure over graves."

"What is the dry and miscarrying hope of all them who are
not in Christ, but confusion and wind? Oh, how pitifully and
miserably are the children of this world beguiled, whose wine
cometh home to them water, and their gold brass and tin ! And
what wonder that hopes builded upon sand should fall and sink !
It would be good for us all to abandon the forlorn and blasted
and withered hope, which we have had in the creature ; and let
us henceforth come and drink water out of our own well, even
the fountain of living waters, and build our hope upon Christ
our Rock. But, alas! that that natural love which we have to
this borrowed home that we are born in, and that this clay city,
the vain earth, should have the largest share of our heart ! Our
poor, lean, and empty dreams of confidence in something besides
God are no further excursive than up and down the noughty
and feckless creatures. God may say of us as he said (Amos vi.
13), 'Ye rejoice in a thing of nought.' Surely we spin our
spider's web with pain, and build our rotten and tottering house
upon a lie, and falsehood, and vanity."—RUTHERFORD.

Fruitless Toil ;

OR,

A WORD TO THE GAY, THE GUILTY, AND THE WISE.

" Simon Peter saith unto them, I go a fishing. They say unto him, We also go with thee. They went forth, and entered into a ship immediately ; and that night they caught nothing. But when the morning was now come, Jesus stood on the shore : but the disciples knew not that it was Jesus. Then Jesus saith unto them, Children, have ye any meat? They answered him, No. And he said unto them, Cast the net on the right side of the ship, and ye shall find. They cast therefore, and now they were not able to draw it for the multitude of fishes."—John xxi. 3—6.

THIS world is a place of fruitless toil; for men are not willing to be instructed. Like the disciples of old, they toil over the sea of life in the dark, fishing for happiness as they go, but generally in vain. Being unwilling to profit by the wisdom of those who have toiled over the sea before them, their net is mostly found on the *wrong*

2

side of the vessel, while they are quite ready to
throw the blame of their numerous failures on
anything and everybody rather than themselves.
Let us, however, endeavour to gather from the
interesting narrative above recorded, those instructions which it is calculated to impart, and which,
through the Divine blessing, may save us from
some of those great mistakes which have transformed the lives of many into one scene of disappointment and sorrow.   We will notice the fruitless toil, the Divine Teacher, and the miraculous
draught.

THE FRUITLESS TOIL. "*I go a fishing,*" *said
Peter.*   And, " Come," says the jovial man to his
boon companions, " Come, let us go and have
some sport to-night.   Away with melancholy:
life is the time to be happy and gay;" and so
away they go to fish for happiness upon the sea
of worldly pleasure.   The night is dark, but their
minds are darker; they have heard that this sea
has its rocks, and is liable to storms, and that
many a goodly ship has been wrecked there, but
what care they; fish they will, and so they toil
all night.   And when the morning comes, what
have they taken?   Answer, ye devotees of pleasure.; let conscience speak; must not your reply
be that of the disciples of old, " We have toiled
all night and taken nothing;" or, worse, that the
dog-fish of weariness and a guilty conscience is
your only reward.

And "I go a fishing," says another. "Come, friends." Alas! one sinner makes many. Their destination? the sea of strong drink. And what result? Answer, ye daring voyagers, ye storm-tossed, weary labourers who have hitherto escaped its boiling waves; withered and blasted, it is true, —scarce men, yet speak. You will not; then God *shall*;—hear what He says your toil *shall* bring: the sea can yield no more. "Who hath woe? who hath sorrow? who hath conten-tions? who hath babbling? who hath wounds without cause? who hath redness of eyes? They that tarry long at the wine; they that go to seek mixed wine. Look not thou upon the wine when it is red, when it giveth his colour in the cup, when it moveth itself aright. At the last it *biteth like a serpent*, and *stingeth like an adder*." And is it for this serpent you will toil all night? that it may sting thee to eternal death, and de-stroy thee in body and soul? And is it to catch *this*, that wife and child, home and friends, are forsaken? Can it be? is it possible? what dread-ful infatuation is this? O temerous voyager, flee from this dreadful sea; thy little bark once upset, thou art lost, for ever lost! O open thine eyes, look around thee: observe how swift the eddying current flows toward yonder rocks—that dread abyss! See, drifting all around thy course, the wrecks of many a gallant vessel, which, like thy own, once proudly danced o'er the surging waves,

buoyant with life, and health, and joy, but now,
alas! no longer seen. O daring fisherman, take
heed! Call now on God for help! nor trust thyself upon the waves of this mad sea again.

And who is that with wan, pale face, and anxious look——a burden, too, tied to his back. He
sighs, and weeps, and labours on. Anon! he
stops and tries to shake his burden off, then starts
afresh; but all in vain. The sea of error is his
goal; and see, he has arrived; and mark how
hard he toils to fish up mercy from the secret
deeps of that dark, gloomy, ever-heaving sea.
How anxiously he strives, all through his dismal
night of sorrow, for pardon and peace of conscience—rest. Alas! he finds them not. Numbers, with him, cast in their nets. The sea is
deep, but yields them nought. Poor man, his
constant draught is disappointment. He watches
other boats, and follows in their wake: they are
strong and confident, and *seem* to catch all they
require; but he takes nought. Still from his lips
the doleful words oft fall, "I've toiled all night
and taken nothing." Yet, o'er the waters of that
troubled sea, the voice of mercy rolls: "Believe,
and peace is yours." It cannot be, he thinks,—
Believe! what, leave off my work; do nothing!
Have all I want for nothing! what idle words
come on the breeze! And so he bends his burdened back down to his oar, "I will have peace,"
"I *must* have peace," he says, while from his eyes

the tears roll down. Poor man, the sea of error cannot yield thee aught to feed thy soul!

And mark yon toiling missionary as he stands weeping in the midst of that degraded band of heathens: why does he weep? He has laboured these many years, and taken nothing. It has been a long, sad night of toil; no solitary star of hope has cheered him; not one of those encompassed by his toil and prayer has bowed to the sceptre of the Prince of Peace, or opened his hard heart to welcome His embrace. And why this failure? He thought the people being so depraved, he had better educate them first—create a moral sense— and *then* make known to them the joyful tidings of a Saviour's death; and hence this disappointment.

How trying to the mind is fruitless toil; but how needful is it to show us our faults, and prepare us to receive the blessing of the Lord when it comes!

THE DIVINE TEACHER. " *But when the morning was now come, Jesus stood on the shore.*"—It is ever morning when Jesus visits His disciples. However dark the night, when He appears the light gets through the clouds, and the morning breaks. O what a bright morning broke upon the dark night of human sorrow at the Incarnation, when Jesus robed Himself in frailty, and for the first time placed His foot upon the shores of this guilty, wrecked, and storm-tossed world!

2*

And oh, what a bright morning will burst upon
the vision of the perfected just, when, standing
upon that sea of glass which John saw in Apoca-
lyptic vision, they behold their glorified Lord:
when, the full fruition of their hopes being realised, their sun shall no more go down, the days
of their sorrow having for ever passed away.

" *He stood on the shore.*"—He was not far from
them. And, ye toiling ones, who have long
been fishing for happiness upon the troubled sea
of worldly gain and pleasure, know that He who
can instruct you how to take the prize is not far
from you; hear His voice, as He expostulates with
you: "Wherefore," saith He, "do ye spend
money for that which is not bread? and your
labour for that which satisfieth not? Hearken
diligently unto me, and eat ye that which *is*
good, and let your soul delight itself in fatness."

" *But the disciples knew Him not.*"—Their
greatest Friend was unknown to them. And be
assured of this, ye sons of fruitless toil, although
the world may smile upon the labour of your
hands, and praise your deeds, and laud your name,
as yet your best Friend is to you unknown.

But though the disciples knew Him not, He
knew them. The night was not too dark for Him
to see them, and mark their toil. And thus, even
now, His omniscient eye surveys the sea of life.
Each little bark He beholds in which His disciples ride, and struggle hard, with many a sigh

and tear, to take enough to meet their wants, until, the voyage being over, they reach the haven
of their hopes.

"*And He stood upon the shore, and He said,
Children, have ye any meat?*"—And thus from
the distant shores of eternity speaks the Great
Teacher now through His truth, and to each
anxious labourer on the sea of life He puts this
question, "Have ye any meat?" Answer, ye *aged*
men, who many years have toiled 'mid stormy seas,
to fill the ship with this world's merchandise, your
only aim: say, Have ye any meat? What! has the
soul been starved? is there no crumb on board to
feed a better hope when storms and tempests
come? What! must you answer "No?" O shame!
How long shall folly claim thy hoary locks, and
fruitless toil hold fast thy withered form, and point
thoughtless youth to thee as his patron, while death
stands by to snatch thee from thy oar, and hell im-
patient waits and opens wide her mouth to take
thee in!

To you, *young man*, no less the Saviour speaks.
Your boat is gay—the sea of pleasure bright—your
sails well spread to catch the gale prosperity now
sends. And what have you? Come, trifler, speak!
God puts the question: you will not answer. You
must some day; better speak now; confess the
truth. There is much display: and is that all?
what saith the *soul?* Your angling rod, your silver
line, and silken nets, have taken nought—have

really brought no satisfaction home. The mind still craves for that you cannot take, with all your sails outspread and nets employed. And so from *you* a negative must come,—" I have no food."

And thou, too, ancient man, with stooping gait and thoughtful mien, and boat well laden too with ancient " saws and modern instances,"—must *you* confess at this late hour your cargo-emptiness? —no meat ! a shoal of doubts fished from the abysses of scepticism, which now you doubt ? rich dainty food, O flourishing condition, wise man! And can it be, O sage philosopher, past now thy threescore years and ten, that with thy nets of metaphysical lore all logically devised, and all thy toil, oft faint and weary, to drag them through the sea of speculation, they bring thee this result— that now the eye is dim, the ears are nearly closed, and o'er the sky dark clouds appear, while in the dim uncertain distance looms the lee-shore death— in answer to the question, put by lips infallible, if thou hast aught on board to meet thy wants just now, must even *you* reply, " I have no meat ; I know not whence I come, or whither I go!" Alas! poor man, and is this all that we can write upon thy coffin lid,—hast thou so laboured that if truth wrote thy epitaph it must stand thus :—

> Here lies a learned fool, who toiled
> All through his life to catch a negative,
> And have the bliss of dying in the dark?

THE MIRACULOUS DRAUGHT. *"And Jesus said, Cast the net on the right side of the ship, and ye shall find. They cast therefore, and now they were not able to draw it for the multitude of fishes."*—See what faith in the words of Christ will do. They had toiled all night in their own way, and taken nothing; while in a few moments' labour, in accordance with the instructions of Christ, and lo! the net breaks. And when Jesus speaks to the guilty and self-condemned sinner, tells him what to do, and gives him the power to do it, O what a change transpires! and how richly is he blessed! and what a shoal of blessings come pouring into the soul, until the man so favoured is compelled to exclaim, Lord, it is enough! and his little bark is liable to be wrecked, not upon the rocks of despair, but of over-much joy. Then, indeed, is fulfilled the gracious declaration, " In that day thou shalt say, O Lord, I will praise thee, though thou wast angry with me: thine anger is turned away, and thou comfortest me." And the man so favoured exclaims, " I will greatly rejoice in the Lord, my soul shall be joyful in my God; for he hath clothed me with the garments of salvation, he hath covered me with the robe of righteousness, as a bridegroom decketh himself with ornaments, and as a bride adorneth herself with jewels." And, when Jesus teaches His servants how to throw in the gospel net, how great is their success! And how speedily do those who have laboured for

happiness in vain reach the spring-head of bliss
when made willing to take Him for their guide.

> "Then come all ye weary,
> And ye heavy laden,
> Lend a glad ear to your Saviour's call :
> Fearing or grieving,
> Yet humbly believing,
> Rest, rest to your souls He'll freely give all.

> " How easy His yoke is!
> How light is His burden!
> But what He suffered no language can tell.
> His grief in the garden,
> To purchase our pardon,
> His pangs on the cross to save us from hell."

From the whole we may learn, that all our
efforts in reference to this world and that which
is to come, without the blessing and presence of
Christ, will only issue in disappointment and
sorrow; at the same time that our past failures
need not unduly discourage us if they do but
lead us to look more simply and exclusively to
Him who is ever ready to instruct and bless His
people, and whose word is sufficient to insure the
success of every enterprise.   And while the fruitless toil of the past may well humble us, it should
also admonish us, and lead us not to look to ourselves or our circumstances, not to speculate, but
obey Him who has said, "Look unto me, and be
ye saved, all the ends of the earth; for I am
God, and there is none else."

" Return, return,
Poor long-lost wanderer, home!
With all thy bitter tears,
Thy heavy burdens, come!
As thou art, all sin and pain,
Fear not to implore in vain:
See, the Father comes to meet thee,
Points to mercy's open door,
Words of life and promise greet thee,
Oh, return, and weep no more!

" Return, return,
From all thy crooked ways!
Jesus will save the lost,
The fallen He can raise.
Look to Him who beckons thee
From the cross so lovingly;
See His gracious arm extended,
Fear not to seek shelter there,
Where no grief is unbefriended,
Where no sinner need despair.

" Return, return!
From all thy wanderings, home!
From vanity and toil,
To rest and substance, come!
Come to truth from error's night,
Come from darkness unto light,
Come from death to life undying,
From a fallen earth to heaven,—
Now, on Jesus' grace relying,
Haste to take what God has given!"

" Faith is the brightest evidence
Of things beyond our sight;
Breaks through the clouds of flesh and sense,
And dwells in heavenly light."

He who believes the truth, shall realise the *power* of truth, and, by the work which it does *within*, will ever be guided to its source *without* : to HIM who is the way, and the truth, and the life.

" You rely on your instinctive sense of the beautiful, as a safe and competent guide, when the question respects the beauty of an object ; you rely on your instinctive sense of the right, as a fit and adequate criterion, when the question relates to the morality of an action : and why not equally trust to your instinctive feeling of the true for a sound and reliable verdict in reference to the credibility of a narrative ? That fine moral tact, by which we distinguish between the genuine and spurious, has been styled the *antennæ* of the mind, and most aptly ; for, like *antennæ*, it possesses a nicety of discrimination, which often renders it a safer and more certain guide than direct reasoning. In our reasonings, a false step at the commencement sends us far astray ; but in gathering up the inductions of the moral sense, we feel our path as we proceed, and at every step get so much nearer to truth and certainty." " *The Life of Jesus its own Witness.*" By the Rev. J. M. M'CULLOCH, D.D.

" All the profoundest truths are *felt* out, the deep glances into truth are got by LOVE."

The Midnight Disciple;

OR,

A GUIDE TO FAITH.

" The same came to Jesus by night."—John iii. 2.

MANY centuries ago, a timid, half-doubting disciple, availing himself of the darkness of night, issued forth from his dwelling-place to seek an interview with the King of kings. The darkness which surrounded his steps, as he pursued his way, well symbolised the sable cloud which covered his mind. Mysteries there were which excited his anxious thoughts, and drew his tardy steps towards the great but unknown Teacher of Israel.

A wonderful sight was presented to this visible universe on the night that this inquiring man found his way into the presence of the Son of God, to give utterance to his perplexities, and fetch wisdom from the lips of the despised Nazarene. Strange that the Creator and the created should thus be brought into visible converse with each other; that He who dwelleth in light which no man can approach unto,—whom no man hath seen, nor can see,—should so veil His glory beneath our nature, that a sinful man could gaze upon His face, and receive instruction immediately from His lips;—that, His greatness being equal to our littleness, He should cover and yet reveal Himself through our humanity, making it not only the temple of His Godhead, but the infallible oracle of those Divine communications which alone can guide the mind to peace and rest.

What Christian mind is there which has not gazed with intense interest upon this scene! Here we behold the great and self-existent Eternal,—that august Being whom the heaven of heavens cannot contain, whose omnific word spoke all things into existence, and who sustains them by His almighty power, clothed in the robes of human frailty,—A MAN among the children of men,—and so completely one with us does He appear, that a poor, guilty, erring· creature is not afraid to approach Him. Who now shall say that God is unwilling to commune with man, or that He has left him, like an orphan, to wander through His universe? that He has no concern for his intellectual and moral manhood? Behold the fountain of heavenly wisdom now flows at his feet, and pours forth its fruitful streams to purify and bless. Through human lips God speaks to man, and through our finite words His thoughts distil like the descending dew upon the seeking heart. Oh, favoured Nicodemus! privileged to hear the voice which never erred, to gaze upon that form which heaven adores; to mark that golden urn in which God's mind lay hid, those moving lips from which God's love distils in words more sweet than honey from the melting comb.

And yet this man came to Christ by night; he skulked into His presence like a thief; he fain would steal instruction from His lips, and take the bread of life by stealth. Oh, shame! methinks his echoing steps might well have waked the dead to frown upon him as he passed along, the shadows of the night refuse their aid, and heaven's own sun shoot forth his rays to spread his shame. Ashamed of Him who left His throne to reach his heart, to take the veil of darkness from his mind, and pour the balm of heaven into his bleeding wounds! And yet this man was not despised, he did not seek in vain. He was not harshly spurned away; his cowardice called forth no frown upon the Saviour's brow, nor did his ignorance excite a laugh. The Teacher whom he sought was great, and wise, and holy, and infallible,— and because He was all this, this timid scholar found a Friend, and for the first time heard the greatest truths which ever fell from mortal lips. Like as a little child with trembling and uncertain steps strives to reach its parent's knees, or struggles to pronounce its parent's name, so doubting

and uncertain Nicodemus ventured forth to reach
the fountain of Eternal Truth. He did not find
that fountain closed because he staggered towards
it in the dark. He was not sent away without
one drop to cool his feverish thirst. He asked,
and he received more than his prayers embraced,
or his poor finite mind could grasp. Of the great
Prophet of his people it had been written, "He
shall not break the bruised reed, nor quench the
smoking flax." Nicodemus proved this promise
true, and by his very fears and doubts instructs
us,—his timid steps may guide us to the Truth.
*It is better to come to Christ in darkness than not at
all.* It is sad to be ashamed of that which fills
the angels with joy, to fear it should be known
we sit at Jesus's feet. The argosy that would
return freighted with rich treasures from the East
must pass through many storms, and plough her
way through surging seas, not only when the light
of day falls on her prow, and gentle zephyrs fill
her sails, but when the night hangs up her sable
curtains o'er the sky, and the straining eye in vain
would catch the smallest ray to cheer the dark
void, to guide the uncertain course over the vast,
mysterious waste of waters. Would she reach
the port of safety, "Onwards," must be the cry,—
mid storm and sunshine, by day and night; and
so the soul in quest of truth, though often hard
beset by sin, darkness, and temptation, by difficulties which, like an adamantine chain, threaten

to bind the soul to the bleak, barren rock of unbelief, must still cry "Onwards," in faith and
prayer, coming to God, crying to Him for light;
must still press forwards to the great central
luminary of eternal truth,—the Christ of God,—
the haven's mouth of Deity,—through which the
ocean of truth pours itself forth, to fertilise and
bless the soul;—the great Light fixed in the steady
heavens of God's Word,—the Christ of God; He
who *is God*, and therefore can understand thee,
seeker after truth,—and succour thee, benighted
traveller, seeking for this gem; despair not, for He
is *equal to all* the strange, mysterious wants of thy
strangely disordered, guilty, and necessitous soul,
—thy subtle thoughts,—the intricate coil of reasoning which draws thy soul hither and thither, until
thy mind, like the troubled sea, can get no rest.
And He is *man;* mysterious truth, but true; and
He can feel for the struggling soul, its pains and
weakness, its hopes and fears. Oh, let thy soul
cry after Him, as cries the helpless infant for its
mother's breast,—come thou to Him in prayer,—
be willing to be taught: in coming to Him thou
wilt find thy doubts forsake thee,—the night of
unbelief will pass away; each prayer, like the
steps of Nicodemus when he went forth to seek
Christ, will bring thee nearer to peace and
rest.

The very exercise of faith and prayer will bring
thee sublimest evidence of the divinity of Him at

whose feet thou dost sit; "For whosoever *doeth* the doctrine shall know that it is of God." "To him that overcometh, will I give to eat of the hidden manna;"—*give to eat*, thus conquering thyself by coming to Jesus—the hidden elements of thy moral constitution, beneath the touch of God's omnipotent Spirit, shall develop themselves, and thou shalt rejoice with joy unspeakable and full of glory. While pride and self are thus placed beneath thy feet, the Holy Comforter will fill thy heart with the honey of God's love, and this initial victory of thy infant faith shall be but the first of a series which shall bring incontrovertible evidence of the Truth to thee, and lift thee higher and higher, even to the very throne of God; where, crowned with His loving-kindness, a son thyself, among His sons and daughters, thou shalt sing with them, "Victory, through the blood of the Lamb!" Then, in the clear sunlight of eternity, with eye undimmed by prejudice or sin,— thou shalt see the spreading lines of Truth, no longer dark, broken, intricate, but converging each to one bright centre—Christ; in whose glorious face wisdom shall still unveil herself, and still enchain and ravish thine unwearied spirit, and conduct thee to still loftier flights, while in all the soaring grandeur of thy blissful and exalted destiny thou shalt thyself appear as a ray flung off from the great centre of Eternal Truth, a marvellous exponent of the divine perfections, upon which even the intelligences of heaven shall look with wonder, instruction, and delight.

Art thou, then, reader, willing thus to lose thyself at the feet of Christ, that thou mayest be truly found—willing to try God's method—to *love* the truth that thou mayest learn the truth? God commands thee thus to learn it, thus to be satisfied—convinced. Wilt thou pronounce an opinion before thou hast tried His prescription? What wouldst thou think of one who, while refusing properly to adjust an optical instrument to the required focus, declared the instrument to be worthless and incapable of manifesting the objects which he desired to behold? And what are we to think of the honesty of those who, while professing to be anxious to know the truth, will not obey those instructions, through the observance of which it is made to appear? A poor man, well known to us, who had wandered for many years in the mazes of infidelity, on returning home one night, by chance opened his Bible; his eye fell upon the passage, "If any man lack wisdom, let him ask of God, who giveth liberally, and upbraideth not." The thought struck him that he had never complied with this command, and he thought he would try it;—he prayed, he adjusted the instrument *before* he looked at the object; the result was conviction, rest, peace,—he became a Christian.

Is the reader perplexed as to the truth? turn,

then, for a time, from the schools of disputation :
see here a more excellent way;—practise the truth
and believe it,—believe it, and thou wilt love it.
A poor, illiterate countryman knows more of
natural life, by the regular performance of the
functions of life, than the angels who are not so
incarnated in flesh and blood, however great
their reasoning powers, or transcendent their
celestial logic. And so, reader, in coming by
prayer to the feet of Jesus, and seeking for divine help to conform thyself to His words, thy
mind will gain more light, and thy heart more
rest, than all thy reasoning can bring. Be mo-
dest, then—rise and obey.

> In Thee my heart, O Jesus, finds reposo;
>   Thou bringest rest to all that weary are.
> Until that day-spring from on high arose,
>   I wandered through a night without a star·
>   My feet had gone astray
>   Upon a lonely way:
> Each guide I followed failed mo in my need;
> Each staff I leaned on proved a broken reed.
>
> Then, when in mine extremity to Thee
>   I turned, Thy pity did prevent my prayer;
> From that entangling maze it set me free,
>   And quickly loosed my heavy load of care;
>   Gave mo the lofty scope
>   Of a heaven-centred hope,
> And led me on with Thee, a gentle guide,
> Thither, where pure immortal joys abide.
>
> Thou art the great completion of my soul,
>   The blest fulfilment of its deepest need;

When self-surrendered to Thy mild control,
It enters into liberty indeed:
.   Thy love, a genial law,
Its every aim doth draw
Within its holy range, and sweetly lure
Its longings toward the beautiful and pure.

Thy presence is the never-failing spring
Of life and comfort in each darker hour;
And, through Thy grace benignly ministering,
Grief wields a secret, purifying power.
'Tis sweet, O Lord, to know
Thy kindredness with woe;
`Sweeter to walk with Thee on ways apart,
Than with the world, where heart is shut to heart.

For Thee eternity reserves her hymn;
· For Thee earth has her prayers, and heaven her vows
Thy saints adore Thee, and the seraphim,
Under Thy glory, stoop their starry brows.
Oh, may that light divine
On me still clearer shine—
A power, an inspiration from above,
Lifting me higher to Thy perfect love!

JAMES D. BURNS.

"Saviour Prince ! enthroned above,
Repentance to impart;
Give me, through Thy dying love,
The humble contrite heart.
Give, what I have long implored,
A portion of Thy love unknown:
Turn and look upon me, Lord,
And break my heart of stone."

"How adorable is that grace of God in Jesus Christ, which hath not only given us the doctrine of repentance, but by His Spirit gives the very grace itself! He puts no trust in our own powers of understanding, will, affections, natural conscience, reason, or morality; but only in His own Spirit and grace in His Son. Nor doth He accept our repentance upon its worth, value, and perfection; but wraps it up in the rich robes of the righteousness of the Lord Jesus Christ, and so it is pleasing in His sight. So He does not lessen or derogate from the graciousness of His Gospel in imposing such a duty, but He magnifies it, by giving so high and admirable a grace and divine power within us."—Psa. lxxx. 3; Job xv. 15; Jer. xxxi. 18, 19.

BEVERLEY.

The Look of Christ;

OR,

HOW TO REPENT.

" And the Lord turned and looked upon Peter. And Peter went out and wept bitterly."—Luke xxii. 61, 62.

AND what a look was that! The eye has told much, eloquently, and well; but never, amid all the tragic scenes of this world's history, did it ever tell out a tale so full of love and sorrow as now. No words could ever have uttered half so well what the eye of Christ so silently *looked* into the heart of his faithless but still loving disciple. This impulsive man had once asked leave of his Lord to walk towards Him on the bosom of the sea, and but for the strong hand of the Saviour would have been drowned; and now, like a loving but inexperienced child, he has followed the Redeemer to the very margin of the dreadful storm about to burst upon his head, and a few of its drops having fallen upon His spirit, under the

influence of terror and with oaths and curses he
denies his Lord.

And what will the Saviour do? He stands in
the midst of an infuriated throng; His body is
still crimsoned over with the bloody sweat which
His anguish in the garden had pressed from His
pores; He is gradually approaching the dread
climax of His grief; the savage yells of men
thirsting for His blood fill His ears; the crown
of thorns is near; His spirit is already crucified;
a dark cloud is coming over the face of His God,
as He is about to pay into the hands of divine
Justice the dread price which is to secure the
salvation of myriads. Under such circumstances,
can anything but His great work arrest His attention? With a heart thus surcharged with grief,
at such a time, can He even for a moment turn
away from Himself? Sinking in deep waters,
can He look away from them? Yes. He hears a
voice, oaths, and curses! He sees a timid sheep
rushing towards the burning lake, and, with the
very dogs of hell seeking to tear His flesh, He
goes forth to the rescue—"*He turned and looked
upon Peter.*" Well, what of that? He looked
upon others; yes, but they *saw* nothing. There
was *meaning* in His look. Peter had seen those
eyes before; he had beheld them beaming love
and mercy upon the poor and wretched, and
filled with tears by the unbelief of His people;—
he knew they had watched for him when he

slept; he had studied their utterances through many a changing scene; they had been welcome to him as the light of heaven, and he had never seen them reflect aught but purity and love; and hence their influence over his soul,—he wept. Ah! well he might; the eyes of Jesus filled his eyes with tears; oh, what a tale of ill-requited love they poured into his bursting heart!

But Jesus "*turned* and looked." Ah Peter! thou didst sadly fall; but, bad as thou wast, thou couldst not deny thy Lord to His face. His back was towards thee doubtless, but not His heart; and hence when He hears thy voice, though but to deny Him, He will *turn* and look. He knew it would be enough; He had but to *look*, and thou must weep. He felt thy heart was near to His, though oaths were upon thy lips. He knew the pangs which thy words brought to His heart would seize upon thy own, and He had only to look to bring them forth. Peter had heard the lips of Christ speak eloquently; but oh, the meaning this look of Christ brought to his heart now that he had proved false to his better self and his Lord!

"He *wept.*" Ah, yes, those eyes brought to his mind the day when first they smiled a welcome as he forsook all to follow Christ, and quickened memory to think of what he had said: "Lord, I am willing to go with Thee both to prison and to death."

4

He " wept *bitterly.*" Ah, well he might. Those eyes,—oh, what reproof, what cowardice, what base ingratitude, he saw reflected there;—himself! what more could he need to add bitters to his tears? He thought upon the past,—oh, what a past! what numerous kindnesses! what proofs of love! what pity and patience! Yet there he stands, that loving, faithful Friend; lone, sad, neglected, and despised; and, alas! denied by him! O memory! awaked by the hand of love, how many and how bitter are the griefs thou bringest to a sinner's heart! How painful to count up the favours of a Friend despised!

"He *looked.*" Yes, and there was sorrow in his eyes, ah, how deep! They seemed to speak and say, Is this thy kindness to thy friend? My heart is deeply pierced just now; must you too make a wound? My foes are strong and many; will you too lend them aid? They are about to crucify me; will you too drive the nails? See, here's my brow; must it have thorns from *you ?*— and "Peter wept." That look made him a man of sorrows, and in the secret chambers of his soul, henceforth, whenever he shall look within, he will see that Man whom he denied,—who in the silent majesty of His awful grief, as there He stands, still looks upon him, and, as often as He looks, bids him to weep.

And there was love, too, in this look. Ah! but for this poor Peter must have died. It was as though the eyes of Jesus said, "What! is this from thee? Peter—*my child*—from thee? What, thou, my own Peter! Ah, well, I hate thy sin, but love thee still; and still to save thee I will die." Oh, had there not been love in the heart of Jesus, He would not have looked; and had not Peter perceived that gaze, he never would have wept. The eyes of Jesus looked into his soul, and from its secret depths welled forth the fruitful streams of tenderness and sorrow for his sin.

And nothing but the love of Christ will melt the heart. Repentance gushes from the heart of Christ, lives neath the beamings of His eyes, and grows beneath the shadow of His cross. Reader, is repentance thine? remember that without it all must perish. How important, then, that thou shouldst look upon Him whom thou hast pierced, and mourn; but let us not forget that the love of Christ will single out its own, though in a crowd and bound by sin. If, therefore, thou hast been led to mourn over and forsake thy sin, then be encouraged,—Jesus has looked upon thee, even as He did upon Peter; and be admonished by the fall of this great Apostle. Beware of leaning to thy own strength, and look constantly to Jesus to finish the work which His own grace has commenced.

Jesus have I ever wept?
    Has my heart Thy sorrows felt?
Has indeed Thy love revealed
    Made this selfish heart to melt?
Have I ever gazed on Thee,
Sorrowing in Gethsemane?

Gazed, O Lord, I often have,
    Cold and lifeless, I must own;
But, O Lord, Thy word declares,
    All thy saints shall gaze and mourn,—
Mourn and weep while viewing Thee,
Sorrowing in Gethsemane.

True it is I often weep,
    And as oft mistrust each tear,
So deceitful is my heart,
    That, O Jesus, oft I fear
I have ne'er by faith viewed Thee
Sorrowing in Gethsemane.

Here I would not be deceived,
    Lord, my life is in this plea;
For I know Thy saints redeemed,
    Each and all in this agree,
Fellowship they have with Thee,
Sorrowing in Gethsemane.

Knowledge merely, too, is vain;
    All Thy chosen people sip
From thy dolorous cup of woe,
    That they may esteem the bliss
Flowing, holy Lord, from Thee,
Sorrowing in Gethsemane.

'Tis for this, O Lord, I seek ;
  Short of this I would not rest :
This, and this alone, can prove
  That my soul in Thee is blest,
Chosen, known, and loved of Thee,
Sorrowing in Gethsemane.

Many sights men love below
  Grieve, pollute, and pain the eye ;
But there is a sight I know,
  Which can raise and purify,—
'Tis to gaze, O Lord, on Thee,
Sorrowing in Gethsemane.

Here it is my soul would dwell,
  Gaze, and wonder, and adore,
Lost as in a sea of love,
  Bottomless, without a shore,
Weeping, gazing, Lord, on Thee,
Sorrowing in Gethsemane.

This alone I know can break,
  Thaw, and melt the rocky heart,
Free me from the reign of sin,
  Holy peace and joy impart,
Sealed by faith as one with Thee,
Sorrowing in Gethsemane.

" He that lacks time to mourn, lacks time to mend:
Eternity mourns that.   'Tis an ill cure
For life's worst ills to have no time to feel them.
Where sorrow's held intrusive, and turned out,
There wisdom will not enter, nor true power,
Nor aught that dignifies humanity."

A Desert Place;

OR,

THE TEST OF DISCIPLESHIP.

" And he said unto them, Come ye yourselves apart into a desert place, and rest awhile : for there were many coming and going, and they had no leisure so much as to eat."—Mark vi. 31.

ALL the incidents in the life of Christ are pregnant with instruction. His whole life is, indeed, a beautiful panorama of moral beauty and spiritual loveliness. He speaks, and we are enlightened; He moves, and we are instructed. No life like His; and happy the man who is so familiar with it, that each scene of which He is the centre object has been photographed upon his mind by the Spirit of God,—whose memory has become a chamber, the walls of which are overspread with pictures from the life of Jesus, hung up by the fingers of omnipotent Love, for the purification of the affections, and the illustration of important principles. Well would it be for us to imitate the enthusiastic connoisseur, who spares neither labour nor money to procure all the paintings of his favourite master; and seek to have our minds so impressed with every incident in the history of Christ, that wherever we sojourn, there might be within us a spiritual gallery of illustration, to which we could constantly repair for meditation. Observe, believer, the man of taste, the lover of art, how carefully he selects those articles of *vertu* to which his predilections attach value; the antiquary, too, see how he burrows among rubbish, both by night and day, hoping to discover some relic which may illustrate his lore, and assist his inquiries after truth. Let us imitate them; and let our spiritual taste and education appear in a constant study of the inspired biography of Him who is "the altogether lovely." From it may we get materials to adorn our conduct, and facts for the confirmation of our faith. May we ever remember, that Christ is the diamond stone of truth, upon which the law is engraven; and seek to have it set permanently in our affections, that we may walk correctly in the light which it emits, and our lives become attractive exponents of its beauty and power.

We need not dwell upon the literal bearing of the fact above recorded, but shall proceed to make use of it to our spiritual advantage.

The religion of Christ is altogether a practical

religion—a religion of life and influence. The very first step we take under its direction involves an act of Divine power, and is expressive of spiritual perception, feeling, and decision on the part of ourselves. Had our Saviour taught men that they could follow Him in silver slippers and gay attire, retaining the friendship of the world, and leaning upon its help as well as his own, He would have had many disciples; but because He pointed them to a desert, lying between this world and that which is to come, held out to them but little to encourage them which perverted reason could approve, and called upon them to count the cost before they commenced the journey, numbers are driven back, and there are but few of whom He could say, "Ye are they which have continued with Me in My temptation." And as it was in the days of Christ, so is it now; many would like to reach the promised land above, and to eat of its delectable fruits, but the wilderness which *must* be passed turns them aside; nor is the promise that Jesus will accompany them, and give them the victory, sufficient to induce them to go forward. The words of Christ never fail, but they cannot simply venture upon *them;* and their faith is shown to be worthless, by its being conquered by sense. Thus all who hear the Gospel of Christ are by Him tried, and their true state declared. His language is too simple to be misunderstood;

He deceives not by fair speeches, nor hides the rough features of the path of life in a blaze of rhetorical splendour. To all who essay to follow Him, He says, "If any man will come after Me, let him deny himself, and take up his cross daily and follow Me." True it is, He also points to a throne and a crown; but the dreaded cross hides their lustre, and the fear of a desert place in their circumstances drives many back again to the world, who, for a time, seemed to promise well for the kingdom of God. And this, indeed, will ever be the course pursued by those whose first movements towards heaven proceed from mere excitement or impulse, and not from that faith which works by love, and leads those in whom it is implanted to cleave to Christ as their portion, and to follow Him through evil report and good report, whithersoever He may lead.

But does this meet the eye of one who has thus turned His back on Jesus, and refused to follow Him, because it was feared the path might lead to a desert place? What! and is this desert place, which, perhaps, after all, may be but the creation of thy fears, more dreadful than the frown of God? Is it more bleak than the confines of despair? more terrible than His wrath who has said, "But if any man draw back, My soul shall have no pleasure in him?" Is it, indeed, more barren than the burning lava of hell, less prolific in comfort than the stings of a guilty conscience, the death-bed of an apostate, or the regions of darkness destined to be the final dwelling-place of all who are ashamed of Christ, and who, while they would have the crown He gives, despise His cross? Oh, think again before you forsake Him of whose people it is written, " That the wilderness and the solitary place shall be glad for them, and the desert shall rejoice and blossom as the rose." What! shun a desert place with Him of whom it is written, that His smile turns " the shadow of death into the morning!" What! refuse to follow Him who forsook the paradise above, to traverse the cold desert of this world, to seek and to save His wandering sheep; who watered His path with His tears, and, that we might not perish, marked out the path of safety with His own blood! Oh, blush for shame, ye timid disciples, who, like Peter, often follow the Lord "afar off;" and ye who have turned your backs upon Him, oh, return! Hear the kind accents of His voice once more, oh, ye wanderers! " Return, thou backsliding Israel," said the Lord, " and I will not cause mine anger to fall on you; for I am merciful, saith the Lord, and I will not keep anger for ever."

Jesus, then, invites His disciples occasionally to accompany Him into a desert. And how much better to be in a desert place with Him, than in a palace without Him; to have a poor table with Him for a guest, than a rich one if He is absent.

But if Jesus invites His disciples to follow Him
into a desert place, He ever leads the way; and
why does He conduct His disciples into such a
locality?

" *There were many coming and going, and they
had not leisure so much as to eat.*"   Ah, this is it;
there are so many coming and going around us—
too frequently such a crowd of worldly persons
and things—that the still small voice of Jesus
cannot be heard for the noise; and hence it is,
that the disciple often finds "a desert place" in a
chamber of sickness and sorrow. Why, it was
needful: we could not find time, so Jesus would
make time for us; for there must be a cessation
from worldly toil, sufficient at least to eat and
digest our spiritual provisions—to think, to meditate, to pray. There must be times of separation
from the world; periods of holy solitude, when
the truth of the gracious declaration is realised:.
"If a man love Me, he will keep my words, and
my Father will love him, and We will come to
him, and make our abode with him."

Thus the solitude of the desert is required by
the true disciple that he may eat and drink with
Christ; that he may enjoy sweet and holy intercourse with Him; that he may receive especial
tokens of His love; and that his faith may be
increased in His all-sufficiency, faithfulness, and
care. For while false faith, like an exotic, dies
amid the pinching blasts of adversity, true faith

is often nourished by the storms which beat upon
it, and never appears more green and strong than
when it shoots forth amid the winter of tribulation. In the desolation, too, of a desert place,
how sweet are the words of Jesus : words which,
in times of prosperity and ease, have been overlooked, are now pondered over, again and again,
until their important lessons become engraven on
the memory. The promises which before seemed
to be closed against the soul's embrace, now open
their breasts of consolation, for, the mind being
sufficiently humbled, consolation can now be
safely imparted. Oh, how, in the midst of the
thick darkness of a desert place, do the precious
promises of Jesus sparkle like jewels before the
eye of faith; and the Word of God, which
seemed so barren before, now appears like an
orchard full of delectable fruits. But not only
are the words of Christ seen, redolent with meaning, nourishment, and beauty, but Christ Himself.
When surrounded by the gay flowers of prosperity, luxury, and pride, the rose of Sharon
attracts but a passing glance. It is in the solitude
and silence of a desert place, that it commands
the closest attention; and when its hidden beauties are discovered, how welcome is its sweet fragrance to revive and invigorate the soul. It is
said of a certain great orator, that he dug a hole
in the earth in which to study, that his attention
might not be distracted from the object of his

5

pursuit by external objects. And though the
Lord does not communicate grace to His disciples
to make them anchorites, yet does He often iso-
late His people that He may impart such instruction as they will not easily forget. A desert
place, of itself, however, is of no service to the
believer. The presence of Jesus must light up
the scene, and His words must fall like dew upon
the heart, through the gracious influence of the
Holy Comforter, in order to the soul's being profited. In every desert spot, therefore, in our
experience, may we ever seek for the presence of
Christ—a favour never denied to those who
seek earnestly and in faith. This realised, good
will be accomplished in us and by us; for no
place is so barren but that we may be blessed,
and made a blessing. Pride will be more completely subdued; self increasingly crucified; fellowship with a suffering Saviour realised; His
tender and loving spirit will be imparted; while
from these lowlands of famine and spiritual destitution, our steps will be quickened towards our
Father's house, where there is ever bread enough
and to spare—where our sun shall no more go
down, and the days of our sorrow will cease.

Let not, then, the believer be surprised should
his Lord conduct him into a desert place to test
his integrity and prove his love; for thus it was
that the Lord led His disciples of old; and of
Abraham it is written, that "after he was tried he

received the promise." And let not the disciple who may be occupying a desert place now, forget that the Lord can make even it a fruitful spot: fraught with the most hallowed enjoyment of Himself, and pregnant with the most divine instructions which sanctify the soul and fit it for a paradise above. And let those from whose path, in temporal things, at least, a desert place seems at present to be far away, remember, that if the heart becomes cold, and the Lord forgotten; that if their engagements become so multiplied that they have but little time and less disposition to find a secret place for communion with Him whom they profess to love and serve, that the Lord, who is jealous of His glory, and concerned for their welfare, will be sure, sooner or later, to make a desert place for them, where they shall have to mourn their folly, and find time for those acts of devotion which are essential to their spiritual health and comfort: for still it is a truth, " That whom the Lord loveth he chasteneth, and scourgeth every son whom He receiveth." And ye secret disciples, whom wealth and respectability, it may be, have held back from a public profession of the Lord, and a visible identification of yourselves with His humble people, beware, lest He who led His disciples into a desert place of old, should send a rough blast from the wilderness of tribulation to remove your golden impediments, to sweep away your conventional difficulties, and to make you as unmistakable in the public exhibition of your love to Him, as is His determination to be glorified in the conduct of all whom He saves.

BY THE REV. HORATIUS BONAR, D.D.

"Far down the ages, now, her journey well-nigh done,
  The pilgrim Church pursues her way, in haste to reach the
    crown.
  The story of the past comes up before her view;
  How well it seems to suit her still—old, and yet ever new.

'Tis the same story still of sin and weariness,
  Of grace and love still flowing down to pardon and to bless;
  'Tis the old sorrow still—the briar and the thorn—
  And 'tis the same old solace yet—the hope of coming morn.

No wider is the gate, no broader is the way,
  No smoother is the ancient path that leads to light and day,
  No lighter is the load beneath whose weight we cry,
  No tamer grows the rebel flesh, nor less our enemy.

No sweeter is the cup, nor less our lot of ill;
  'Twas tribulation ages since, 'tis tribulation still;
  No greener are the rocks, no fresher flow the rills,
  No roses in the wilds appear, no vines upon the hills.

Still dark the sky above, and sharp the desert air;
  'Tis wide, bleak desolation round, and shadow everywhere;
  Dawn lingers on yon cliff, but O, how slow to spring!
  Morning still nestles on yon wave, afraid to try its wing.

No slacker grows the fight, no feebler is the foe,
  Nor less the need of armour tried, of shield, and spear, and
    bow;
  Nor less we feel the blank of earth's still absent King,
  Whose presence is of all our bliss the everlasting spring.

Thus onward still we press, through evil and through good—
Through pain and poverty, and want—through peril and
    through blood;
Still faithful to our God, and to our Captain true;
We follow where He leads the way, the kingdom in our view."
5*

Take no denial from the lips of love,
  Nor think that silence is a proof of hate,
For Jesus tries the faith he means to bless;
  Be patient, then, and at His feet still wait.

"But what, on second thought, are these merits? Jeremy Taylor tells us, in his life of Christ: Nothing but the innumerable sins which we have added to what we have received. For we can call nothing ours, but such things as we are ashamed to own, and such things as are apt to ruin us. Everything besides is the gift of God; and for a man to exalt himself thereon is just as if a wall on which the sun reflects should boast itself against another that stands in the shadow."

"All that Antinomianism which the orthodox preachers of free grace are falsely charged with lies here, because they maintain that the first thing a convinced sinner is to eye, on his turning to God, is the free grace and mercy of God in Christ for the pardon of sin. Evangelical conviction leads him to a reliance upon Christ, in some degree, of saving faith for the pardon of all his sins; and this faith begets in him a secret hope of pardon, and is the spring of all after sanctification, namely, of mortification, of sin, of repentance, and of all new obedience. Let this be remembered, as the main thing we contend about, that we begin our religion at the grace of God, and do not think to ground our faith in Christ upon any legal preparations or works of our own." (Tit. iii. 5, 6.)   COLE.

The Syrophenician Woman;

OR,

THE SUCCESSFUL APPLICANT.

" And she said, Truth, Lord : Yet the dogs eat of the crumbs which fall from their masters' table."—Matt. xv. 27.

WE have often been struck with the love and courage of Dr. Kane and his party, as recorded in his arctic explorations: travelling mile after mile, dragging a sledge with them over wastes of snow, that they might plant their caches of pemmican and other provisions; that so, if the poor wanderers they were seeking should pass that way, they might be kept from starvation. But how much more affecting is it to contemplate Christ, in the midst of the arctic regions of this world's desolations, travelling hither and thither to deposit by word and example the bread of life. Here and there, now and again, a child of faith would meet Him, like a solitary hesperis, amid the snows of our moral winter, whose beauty and fragrance refreshed him; and such, no doubt, was His experience on meeting with the Syrophenician, whose memorable reply we have cited above; and whose spirit and conduct we would seek to subordinate to our spiritual profit. And we would first notice

HER ZEAL.—She "*came out*" to meet Christ; she was willing to exert herself; she did not wait for Christ to come to her—she went to Him; but how many professing Christians are there who appear too slothful to seek a blessing, even from the hand of God. Through the public ministrations of His Word He showers down His favours; but they are not prepared to make any effort to reach the place where they are so richly and freely vouchsafed; the pearls of truth literally cover their path, but it appears almost too much trouble for them to stoop and pick them up. Alas! for the condition of such; and who can wonder at their poverty? but the day will come when they shall mourn for those privileges which they now despise. This poor woman "*came out;*" she left her home. She had doubtless heard of the fame of Christ, and was willing to put Him to the test. If we would receive a blessing from Christ, we must not be content with simply hearing *of* Him, we must come *to* Him: we must be willing to forsake the world—to be singular, if need be; to part with our prejudices, our crude notions, traditional creeds, darling sins—indeed, with everything which we discover to be opposed to our spiritual progress. For thus speak the lips of love: "Come ye out from among them, and be ye separate, saith the Lord; and touch not the unclean thing; and I will receive you, and I will be a Father unto you, and ye shall be my daughters, saith the Lord Almighty."

Observe, further, that this woman did not come to Christ under the influence of a mere vague curiosity; but to seek a favour from Him. She came intelligently to accomplish a certain object; and were the thousands who go forth merely to hear a preacher's voice year after year, from custom or from habit, but moved to seek an interview with Christ, how soon would our moral petrefactions begin to melt, and the wastes of Zion begin to rejoice and blossom as the rose.

HER FAITH.—She came to CHRIST—she did not go *first* to His disciples, but came direct to Him, and let all who are just beginning to enquire after truth imitate her example: let such, with prayer and supplication, go *at once* to the great Teacher Himself. He invites such. "Take my yoke upon you, and LEARN OF ME," He says, "for I am meek and lowly in heart." Oh, what trouble and perplexities would many have escaped if, at the commencement of their religious career, they had but gone *direct* to Christ as the great Teacher of His people! But they went first to the disciples, forgetful of their Lord, and from

.trusting to the judgment of those who were not competent to guide them, were led from the truth, as well as kept from the enjoyment of that pardon and peace they were so anxious to possess. Let the sincere inquirer, therefore, take heed, and not put the servant in the place of the Master; but search the Scriptures for himself, and pray for the teaching of that gracious Spirit whose especial work it is to take of the things of Christ and show them to His disciples.

Observe, too, *how* this woman came. We are not aware that she had either precept, promise, or example to encourage her: she was " a woman of Canaan;" she had no legal claim to the favour she sought; literally she was not a child of Abraham, *yet she came.* O, what an example to many more favourably circumstanced; and how does her faith reprove their unbelief! Who among those who hear the gospel can say that *they* have neither precept, promise, nor example to encourage them to *come* to Christ; and yet how doubts and fears perpetually rob many of them of their joy. We have no *right* to go to Christ, say they: His precepts, promises, and commands refer to *saints;* we are not such. Then go as *sinners*— go as the poor woman—determine with the poet—

"I can but perish if I go,
  I am resolved to try;
For if I stay away, I know
  I must for ever die."

HER PRAYER.—She cried, "*Have mercy on me, O Lord, Thou Son of David.*" She recognised His dominion and dignity, by calling Him LORD; and also His authority to save as the Messiah of His people. She had learned something of His character, and her trouble furnished her with a prayer; she prayed *earnestly*, too, because her trouble pressed heavily. Real prayer is the offspring of necessity, the child of penury and want. Many come to God's house, and where Christ is preached and dispenses His favours, but are not blessed because they do not pray; they receive not because they ask not; or ask under the influence of mere formality. This poor woman *cried* unto the Lord; she was earnest. "I cried unto the Lord," says the psalmist: many pray who do not *cry* to the Lord. "*Have mercy upon me,*" she exclaimed; no doubt her neighbours had heard of the Saviour as well as herself, but perhaps they had no sorrow in their dwellings, as certainly they had no faith in their hearts; and hence they came not to Him who only can save. It is a sense of their need of mercy which makes men cry to the Lord, which gives eloquence to their words, and dictates those petitions which move the heart, and command the help of Christ.

HER IMPORTUNITY.—"*Jesus answered not a word;*" but she did not despair, but went to His disciples to get them to intercede with their Lord —and in our distresses it is well to seek the

prayer of our brethren ; delay, however, is not
denial with the Lord. "Our time," He tells us,
"is always ready ;" but He will try the faith of
His people ; "*The Lord trieth the righteous.*" If we
would be really blessed of the Lord, the determination of Job must be ours, "*Though he slay me
yet will I trust Him.*" Though our trials should
be severe, and our prayers remain unanswered,
we must continue to pray. We must imitate the
poor woman who came back again and worshipped
Him, saying, "*Lord, help me!*" Let not the
silence of Jesus discourage us, for thus He frequently deals with His people, to constrain them
to more importunity with Him; He delights to
help them, but He loves them to seek His aid,
and to take no denial.

HER HUMILITY AND ARGUMENT.—"*It is not meet
to take the children's bread and cast it to dogs!*"
Why this is worse than silence ; surely, the poor
woman must have thought this a hard speech
from the lips of LOVE. Our Saviour was not
content simply to call her a dog, but in order
to give full force to His rebuff, and to test her
faith, He says, "It is not meet to take the *children's* bread and to cast it to dogs." She would
understand this, however poor and illiterate, for
she was a *mother.* She knew how she felt when
she looked upon a dog, and what were her feelings when she gazed upon her child. She could
appreciate, therefore, the full force of our Sa-

viour's words. "There are some upon whom
He looks as I look upon my child; there are
others upon whom He looks as I do upon a dog;
most assuredly I am among the latter. ' It is not
meet to take the children's bread and cast it to
dogs.' No, it is not meet; how could I bear to
see my child's bread taken from her to be given
to a dog!" What will she do? She understands
Him well. " TRUTH, *Lord!* I am all thy words
imply—a sinful creature—I deserve thy scorn—I
have no claim upon Thy love—I am not a child,
nor have I any right to participate in the blessings of thy chosen. *Truth, Lord!* although thy
words condemn, and all but quench my hope,
still Thou art LORD, and hast *a right* thus to
address me, and to reject my plea: for known to
Thee are all my ways; and all Thy words are
truth. I *am* a dog—be this admitted; wilt Thou
not permit me to use my misery as an argument
with Thee? Do not the dogs eat of the crumbs
which fall from their masters' table?" O misery,
how ingenious art thou! O necessity, thou hast
an eloquence no artifice can counterfeit! Formality never pleaded thus with Christ: hunger
will eat its way through stone walls, and put a
plea into the lips of ignorance itself; want makes
the poor speak well, and gives grace and vigour
to their words. It is said, this woman's country-
men were celebrated for their wit; her daughter's
sufferings doubtless stimulated hers, and taught

6

her how to make an ugly proverb plead her
cause. A burdened heart will frequently brighten
up the mind, and make even the lips of utter
helplessness grow bold. "*Even 'the dogs eat of
the crumbs which fall from their masters' table.'*
Wilt Thou let this privilege be mine? I do not
ask a loaf, but a crumb; what, then, wilt Thou
deny me this? It is but the refuse of thy mercy
I implore: I will not rob thy children, nor will I
take their place; I will sit beneath thy table,
Lord, if I may have a crumb. Most gladly will
I take the dog's place; with joy I'll sit with
them, if I may have their fare—'a crumb.' I
know it is more than I deserve, but oh, a crumb
is life! Mere sinful men will let their dogs have
these; and wilt thou let thy mercy be outdone
by such?" Sweet eloquence of want! Humility,
how forcible thy words! This woman will prevail; have we her spirit? How many a professing Christian would be offended with the language addressed to her, though from the lips of
Christ! What, call us dogs! we are no worse
than others! Reader, be not deceived. What
saith the Word? "But we are all as an unclean
thing, and all our righteousness are as filthy rags;
and we all do fade as a leaf; and our iniquities,
like the wind, have taken us away." Does this
declaration agree with thy experience? Did
Christ call thee a dog, would'st thou respond,
"Truth, Lord?" Hast thou so deep a conscious-

ness of thy depravity, that it would not offend thee, but rather lead thee to turn thy misery into a plea with the Lord, that the crumbs of His mercy might be thine? Oh, remember it is written, that the "poor shall be filled, but the rich sent empty away!" Learn the secret of success with the Lord from the distressed Syrophenician; truly confess thy depravity and guilt, and throw thyself entirely on His unmerited favour alone.

HER SUCCESS.—" *O woman, great is thy faith!*" Scarcely was the admission made when the answer came. And why is the answer to our prayers so frequently delayed? Is it not because the heart is too proud to admit the truth of our condition? The silence of Jesus is the silence of love; He sees that a speedy answer would spoil His work. The heart frequently requires more bruising than we imagine, in order that the truth in open acknowledgment may come freely from our lips.

" *O woman, great is thy faith!*" His rough reply only added to its vigour; His discipline did but develop its latent strength. He knew that it would: the character of her faith was well known to Him when first her cry fell upon His ears; but He would have this appear, that others might be profited by her example. He commended the faith that would not take a refusal. Jesus loves the faith which cleaves to Him in the storm, that strives to grasp His hand when the waves of guilt and sorrow strive to loosen the soul from its

anchor; that will rest upon His word when reason
declares there is no hope, and unbelief gives up all
for lost; a faith that the changes of life cannot
wither, nor despair overcome; that ever exclaims,
"Though He slay me, yet will I trust Him."

"*Great is thy faith.*" And what was the
character of the faith which Jesus commended?
It stood connected with zeal, childlike simplicity,
importunate prayer, profound humility, and unwavering confidence in the ability of Christ to
grant what was sought. If we have such a faith,
though we have not the assurance of faith, and
though we cannot say positively that Christ is ours,
let us take heed that we properly estimate its value,
nor look upon that as a common thing which
brings commendation from the lips of its great
Author.

"*Be it unto thee as thou wilt.*" What a god-
like declaration is this! Her faith had entreated
him as LORD, and He now addresses her as such.
"*Be it unto thee as thou wilt.*" "Satan shall be
dethroned, and thy daughter shall be healed. I
am overcome by thy faith; thy will is mine own,
I throw the reins into thy own hands; my love
grants thy request. O saint, what a God thou dost
serve! O sinner, what a Saviour thou dost despise!"
"*Be it unto thee as thou wilt.*" "Thy faith can
be trusted; it will dictate that which is right."
Illustrious woman! she has conquered the King
of kings and Lord of lords; all the perfections of

Deity now come forth to her help; Omnipotence moves at her bidding to effect her desire, and her will for a time is as the will of God. Even so shall it be with all who come to the Lord possessed of the same faith, and clothed with the same humility; who plead with the same importunity, and wait upon Christ in the exercise of the same grace.

"One Priest alone can pardon me,
  Or bid me 'Go in peace;'
Can breathe that word, 'Absolvo te,'*
  And make these heart-throbs cease.
My soul has heard His priestly voice;
It said, 'I bore thy sins—rejoice!'   1 Pet. ii. 24.

He showed the spear-mark in his side,
  The nail-print on His palm;
Said, 'Look on Me, the crucified.
  Why tremble thus? Be calm!
All power is Mine—I set thee free.
Be not afraid—Absolvo te.'   Isa. xlv. 22.

In chains of sin once tied and bound,
  I walk in life and light;
Each spot I tread is hallowed ground,
  Whilst Him I keep in sight,
Who died a victim on the tree,   ⸻
That He might say, 'Absolvo te.'   1 John i. 7.

By Him my soul is purified,
  Once leprous and defiled;
Cleansed by the water from His side,
  God sees me as a child.
No priest can heal or cleanse but He;
No other say, 'Absolvo te.'   Matt. viii. 3.

* I pardon thee.

6*

He robed me in a priestly dress
  That I might incense bring
Of prayer, and praise, and righteousness,
  To heaven's eternal King.
And when He gave this robe to me,
He smiled and said, ' Absolvo te.'   Zech. iii. 4, 5.

In heaven He stands before the throne,
  The great High Priest above,
MELCHISEDEC '—that name alone
  Can sin's dark stain remove.
To Him I look on bended knee,
And hear that sweet ' Absolvo te.'   Heb. viii. 1.

A girded Levite here below,
  I willing service bring;
And fain would tell to all I know
  Of Christ the Priestly King;
Would win all hearts from sin to flee,
And hear him say, ' Absolvo te.'   1 John ii. 1.

' A little while,' and He shall come
  Forth from the inner shrine,
To call his pardon'd brethren home:
  O bliss supreme, divine!
When every blood-bought child shall see
The PRIEST who said, ' Absolvo te.' "   Heb. ix. 28.

" And I will study to adorn
My heart with meekness under scorn,
    With gentle patience in distress,
With faithful love, that yearning cleaves
To those o'er whom to death it grieves,
    Whose sins its very soul oppress.

When evil tongues, with stinging blame,
Would cast dishonour on my name,
    I'll curb the passions that upstart,
And take injustice patiently,
And pardon, as Thou pardon'st me,
    With an ungrudging, generous heart."
                    PAUL GERHARDT.

The Silence of Jesus;

OR,

HOW TO MEET FALSE ACCUSATIONS.

" But He answered him not to one word."—Matt. xxvii. 14. (*Old Translation.*)

How expressive is silence—"the silence of old ocean resting after storms;" when its hoary heaving bosom is lulled to sleep, its boisterous pealing anthem hushed, and placid and quiet it spreads before the eye a striking picture of qui- escent omnipotence and infinite repose. The silence of night, too, is not less potent in its influ- ence; when the many strings of nature's harp cease their vibrations, and the stars looking down quietly upon us, so soft and subdued in their lustre, seem to invite us for a time to throw aside the depressive cerecloths of mortality, and join with them in sublime and silent awe to muse His praise who made them all. And we read also that there was once "silence in heaven about the

space of half an hour;"—a period when even the
orchestra of glory ceased to yield its notes, and
angels' fingers faltered on the strings of harps
which had never ceased to praise. That silence
must have been *felt:* it was something new; the
sudden stop in the grand chorus of heaven's vast
choir, its myriad harps and voices; how impressive! The angelic tongues all mute; the holy
worshippers filled with expectation, waiting to
learn why *they* must suspend their sweet employ;
what solemn mandate from the eternal throne is
this? what does it mean? How heaven's vast
silence must have startled them! But not the
silence of the slumbering deep beneath its myriad
waves, the voiceless night, or heaven's vast
temple, is so affecting or instructive as the silence
of Him of whom it is written, "*But He answered
not a word.*" He had listened to *many*, and such
words! He was pure, but they made Him vile;
He was true, but they made Him false; He was
God, but they made Him man. But He answered
not a word! The charges cannot affect Him perhaps? He stands impeached for His life: should
His accusers accomplish their purpose, His doom
will be sealed; there are cruel men standing by,
eager to buffet Him; there is a crown of thorns
and a purple robe; a weary journey and a heavy
cross; the rugged nails, and a fearful death!
Yet He utters not a word; perhaps He cannot
speak—has no skill to plead? None so eloquent

as He. Perhaps He knows not how to meet the
rude falsehoods of hell? He is the wisdom of
God. Then why is He silent? Does He not feel
the indictment? More than words can express.
Does He perceive His danger? More clearly
than His persecutors. But He sees also what
they do not—those words of His servant which
they do not understand: "He was oppressed, and
He was afflicted, yet He opened not His mouth:
He is brought as a lamb to the slaughter, and as
a sheep before her shearers is *dumb*, so He opened
not His mouth."

It is this seals His lips; love has brought Him
here to die; love will not let Him speak. In
vain you taunt Him, cruel men; in vain you condemn Him, venal judge! His love will baffle all
your efforts; you may threaten and reproach,
hold up His name to scorn, and even rob Him of
life; but you will hear no complaint, you will get
no reply. He stands before you to suffer, for this
He is prepared; He has counted the cost; He has
come to plead through His deeds, but not for
Himself; to give emphasis to His words, though
not in the vindication of His fame, but in the
salvation of His Church. He will speak for His
people, but He has no words for Himself; He is
dumb in His own cause, though so eloquent in
theirs; and that His words may avail for them
He will give His own blood. Hence, now, He
will not speak, it is His intention to die. He

knows the charges are untrue, but He has prepared no defence. He could defeat His accusers,
but His Church must be saved.

Ah! this is why those lips, so eloquent to
plead the sinner's cause, are silent now; the
tongue of slander cannot make Him speak, for
He will save·His Church, and teach her how to
stand unmoved amid the strife of tongues.

"*He uttered not a word.*"—Can we forget this?
Yes, we can. But let us not: and when the fang
of envy, anxious to wound, gives forth perpetually the poison of misrepresentation; when prejudice, intent to spy defects, pores over each act
and word; when slander makes a target of our
reputation, her darling aim to hold us up to
scorn, then let the silence of those lips which
plead our cause admonish us; and let us strive
to imitate Him, who, though falsely accused,
uttered no angry word; let us seek for grace to
keep, subdue, and guide; so shall our deeds be
our defence, and form a shield malicious words
shall never pierce. While in the ears of calumny, anxious for our ruin, we shall be proclaimed disciples of Him, "who, when He was
reviled, reviled not again; when He suffered, He
threatened not; but submitted Himself to Him
who judgeth righteously."

> "Should envious tongues some malice frame,
> To soil and tarnish your good name,
>   Live it down!

Grow not dishearten'd; 'tis the lot
Of all men, whether good or not:
Live it down!

Rail not in answer, but be calm;
For silence yields a rapid balm:
Live it down!

Go not among you friends and say,
Evil hath fallen on my way:
Live it down!

Far better thus yourself alone
To suffer, than with friends bemoan
The trouble that is all your own:
Live it down!

What though men *evil* call your *good!*
So CHRIST himself, misunderstood,
Was nail'd unto a cross of wood!
And now shall you, for lesser pain,
Your inmost soul for ever stain,
By rendering evil back again?
Live it down!

Oh! if you look to be forgiven,
Love your own foes, the bitterest even,
And love to you shall glide from heaven;
And when shall come the poison'd lie,
Swift from the bow of calumny,
If you would turn it harmless by,
And make the venom'd falsehood lie,
Live it down!"

7

"When we look at our great High Priest in faith, we may look at ourselves (bad as we are) without despair, at our enemies (however many) without fear, at our trials (however great) without repining, and at our duties (however difficult) without discouragement."—*Our Great High Priest,* by JOHN COX.

"Sinners can do nothing but make wounds that Christ may heal them, and make debts that He may pay them, and make falls that He may raise them, and make deaths that He may quicken them, and spin out and dig hells for themselves that He may ransom them. Now I will bless the Lord that ever there was such a thing as the free grace of God, and a free ransom given for sold souls: only, alas! guiltiness maketh me ashamed to apply to Christ, and to think it pride in me to put out my unclean and withered hand to such a Saviour! But it is neither shame nor pride for a drowning man to swim to a rock, nor for a ship-broken soul to run himself ashore upon Christ."—RUTHERFORD.

"He lives, he lives! and sits above,
    For ever interceding there.
Who shall divide us from His love,
    Or what should tempt us to despair!"

Christ and the Demoniac;

NEVER DESPAIR.

" And they come to Jesus, and see him that was possessed with the devil, and had the legion, sitting, and clothed, and in his right mind : and they were afraid."—Mark v. 15.

THIS world is but a huge necropolis, a city of the dead ; it is filled with tombs, among which men wander like the demoniac of old, the sport of sin, and slaves of Satan. Their condition, indeed, is so bad, that it finds but a faint illustration in the history of the poor Gadarene, as above recorded.

This poor creature, it seems, was possessed by a legion of devils : other spirits besides his own had mastered him, and he was their wretched vassal, and compelled to obey. He might have been conscious of his bondage, and frequently have mourned over the fearful servitude by which he was held, without being able to escape from

his thraldom, or to eject his foes. He had also a
companion in misery; so that, if ever he had a
lucid interval, he could fully contemplate himself
as thus reflected, and fully appreciate all the hor-
rors of his condition. And as thus situated, in
his position and conduct, he most forcibly illustrates the condition of many morally before God.
True it is, men are not literally possessed of devils; but all are by nature the slaves of sin, and
led captive by the great adversary at his will.
Of many, too, who boast of their liberty, it is but,
too evident that they are the slaves of corruption:—certain evil tendencies, which they should
have checked, have been fostered until they have
issued in inveterate habits, through the medium
of which, as with so many strong cords, the great
Evil One binds them to 'his chariot wheels, and
drags or guides them whithersoever it pleases
him. Some of them laugh and sing on their way,
like so many demoniacs, making great and noisy
pretensions to freedom; ·while others, conscious
of their degradation, savagely snap at their bonds,
but cannot get free.

Nor was it enough that the demons took possession of these Gadarenes, but they carried them
away from their homes and all the pleasures of
social life. Their friends smiled upon them, but
they smiled not again; they addressed words of
love to them, but they met with no response.
And how frequently does sin cut off men from

social happiness and God! Their Maker smiles
upon them through His works, but they smile not
again; He speaks to them in accents of love
through His Word, but they obey not His voice.

Nor was this all: these poor creatures made
their home among the tombs. And oh, how
many are there, who, although they live in the
midst of a moral paradise, where streams of pure
and innocent pleasures ripple at their feet, and
invite their lips to drink,—live encompassed with
the sweet flowers of every saintly virtue, the rich
odours of which rise perpetually around them,—
nevertheless forsake all to wander amid the paths
of vice, and live comparatively alone amid the
exhalations of moral pestilence and death. O
dreadful solitude! well symbolized by the tombs
among which the poor Gadarene dwelt.

He sometimes changed his position, but it was
ever for a tomb—the cold sepulchre, death beneath him, and corruption around him. Well
did his cold prison-house of the grave shadow
forth the icy desolation of those upon whose
spirits the sweet sun of hope and joy never shines,
and whose eyes are never gladdened by the sweet
flowers of warm-hearted benevolence, cheerfulness, and peace.

It was meet that he should dwell in a charnel-
house whose dead, cold, apathetic heart never
beat responsive to human joy or nature's charms.
Summer came, and threw her smiling progeny

7*

around his path, and Winter beat his icy morsels in his face, but still he heeded not. He was a demoniac.

And in the cold, dreary sepulchre of this demoniac, who does not see the home of dark misanthropy—the arctic regions occupied by those who live for self and sin: cold, cold in heart to God and Christ, and purity and peace? A palace sometimes their home, a sepulchre it is found, for selfishness, has bound them to themselves,—a spot of vile corruption, on which the sun of Jesu's love never shines, and where moral winter ever throws its icy chains around all.

And others, too, hemmed in by deeds of moral turpitude, live on, shut out from heaven's own joys. The slaves of vicious habits, a moral fever spreads around their path, and carries death to all that is good, wherever they come; a walking lazar-house, their moral leprosy shuts them up in dens of infamy, amid the vile. Their home is but a tomb—a dark, cold place, though songs and revelry and thoughtless mirth are often found within. No ray of heavenly light relieves the gloom; no vernal sun of grace appears to make another spring, and cause the vital sap of love to God and holiness to spring forth, or streams of calm domestic joys and filial love and charity to flow. Say now, ye jaded devotees of pleasure, is not all this true? is not your heart a sepulchre, your home a grave? and happiness and peace, are

they not far away? Naked of that which gives
real joy, is not your path, a place of death, vile
and corrupt—of blighted hopes, and pain, and
fruitless toil, and disappointment? Are you not
sad and cheerless, though you laugh? and does
not the cold hand of desolation oft unbidden press
your spirit down, even when it strives to rise?
And, though you turn your head aside, do not the
grave-yard and the tomb too frequently present
themselves, and look you in the face? and the
coffin-lid, the shroud, the gloomy pall, and the
crawling worm, come creeping in between the in-
terludes of your wild mirth, refusing to move at
your behest? and when at night sleep flies the
burning brow, does not the dreaded bar, the awful
Judge, appear? Ye know 'tis even so: your
home is with the dead, ye dwell among the tombs.

And ye, too, who, with look demure and down-
cast eyes, so shake your head as though your
garments were so white that an angel's fingers
would defile them,—are you among the tombs?
"You never did any harm!" What, have you
never sinned? Is not this world your home?
You are respectable; you pay your way, and go
to church ; your neighbours praise you, for you
have done well for yourself; your moral cloak
and Sunday principles have helped you on, and
brought you many customers, and so you think it
well to keep to them, and to abstain from outward
sin. You are a prudent man. Yes; but what of

faith in Christ, His blood and righteousness, internal purity, and hungering after truth? What of love to Christ, His Gospel and people for His sake? What of a daily cross, through sin and self-denying labour to make known the fame of Him who died to save the lost? What of delight in prayer, and holy fellowship with Christ, and constant sorrow on account of sins against His love? You know these things are strange to you. Most prudent man, prudent to bless yourself, and flee the reproach of Christ,—while yet you mourn the follies of the world! Your heart is like a stone to Christ —from it no spring of love wells forth to God and man; the fruits of holy intercourse with Him, through Christ, you never taste; the flowers of faith, and hope, and love throw not their fragrance round your path. Outwardly correct your conduct, it is true, your heart is yet a sepulchre, within which a mass of moral putrefaction lives, with bones of worldly pride and care, and love of self, and ease, and fame, and gold. Mourn for yourself, O man! the plague-spot is within; the man among the tombs is even still *your* archetype.

The Gadarene was cruel to himself, too, fond of cutting himself with stones. How cruel is Satan, and how cruel he makes men to themselves! How favoured those whom grace makes friendly to themselves! With the sharp stones of their own darling sins how frequently do men cut themselves. Well may they exclaim, " My wounds stink and are corrupt, by reason of my foolishness." Could we have seen the poor creature thus wounding his body, how we should have wept, and have entreated him to have had mercy upon himself; and yet with what insensibility do we behold men from day to day busily employed in wounding the soul, the nobler part. How seldom do we mourn over their self-inflicted wounds, although we are persuaded they are bleeding them down to eternal death. May the Lord forgive us, and take away these hearts of stone, and, in mercy to ourselves and others, impart to us more spiritual sensibility and love!

This poor man was also incorrigible in his folly. He had been bound, but it was of no use, he burst the chains; no man could tame him. How obstinate is man, frequently in the perpetration of that which must issue in his own ruin. Down, down to the very marl of hell he will rush, though he tread upon burning embers with naked feet at every step. To the fire which is never to be quenched, and the worm which never dies, he will pass on, though a burning thirst feeds upon his strength, and racks his limbs with pain. To disease and sickness, to days of sorrow, and lone, sad nights, to poverty and pain, to prison and nakedness, the grave, the bar of God, the awful pit, the wailings of the damned, he hastens on. In vain the law puts forth its iron hand and binds its manacles about his limbs, until they fester in

their embrace. In vain it holds up to his view
the prison, the gallows, the grave. In vain his
friends, yea, his own flesh, and sometimes dearly
loved, attempt to hold him back, with cries and
tears entreat him to return, to stop; but all in
vain! On, on, 'mid blasted hopes and broken
vows, mid open graves and lowering clouds, like
the wild hurricane he passes by. The thunders
of a broken law fall on his ears, the distant mut-
terings of Almighty wrath; the vivid flash of
hell's own fire darts ever and anon across his
path, and seems to burn his very clothes — he
heeds not; but still 'tis on, on, until, if mercy
stay not, in one dread moment, with one dread
shriek, he disappears like as a spark falls into the
surging ocean and is gone! O incorrigible sinner!
see here thy destiny, if still thou spurn the warning voice of God. And wilt thou not tremble?
Oh, why this dreadful haste to die? Is hell indeed a place so dear to thee, that thou wilt break
the laws of God and man to reach it? Oh, why
this suicidal toil to curse thyself? Is sin so sweet
a draught to thee, that thou wilt sell all present
joy, and face an angry God to get it to thy lips?
Oh, from the depths of thy dark heart now cry
to God! Steel not thy soul against Omnipotence.
True, thou hast laid thy head upon the lap of sin,
and she has sold thee to thy foes, to make them
cruel sport; still heed not, but in the hour of this
thy dread necessity look up, and seek by prayer

to grasp His strength whose word omnipotent loosened the Gadarene, and He will hear and save.

Of the appearance of this poor demoniac we can form but a very feeble conception. Imagine a creature in a state of shameful nudity—his flesh all lacerated and torn, his skin covered with dirt, while his flowing blood declares his wounds but recently made—his hair, all wild and dishevelled, floating on the breeze—his beard hanging matted and filthy upon his breast—his clenched teeth and staring eyes expressing the most savage determination. Imagine you see him rushing hither and thither, that you hear his loud yells as he cuts himself with stones, or pursues some imaginary form, upon whom he hopes to expend his rage; failing in his design, observe how he casts himself upon the ground, foaming with anger, and uttering the most horrid imprecations, or exhausted by the violence of his feelings; mark his wan, worn face, as in hopeless agony he wanders up and down, wringing his hands and weeping over his hapless destiny. What a sight! and how gladly we turn from so offensive an object. But not half so offensive to your eye is such a one, as is the man who is living under the influence of sin, and fully conformed to Satan. Such is said to be wretched, and miserable, and poor, and blind, and naked. The state of man by nature, indeed, is such, that the condition of

this poor Gadarene literally is but a faint picture
of his state spiritually; and hence he is said to be
a child of wrath and slave of Satan.

But even of this poor Gadarene we read, that
he was observed sitting at the feet of Jesus,
clothed, and in his right mind.   Well might
those who saw him be astonished.   Why, what
mysterious power has mastered his foes?   How
came he there? what did it involve?   A visit
from Jesus, of whom it is recorded, that He went
into the coast of Gadara, though infested by such
characters.   He was not afraid to do so, though
He knew that Satan had his strongholds there,
and that some whom he had mastered were very
fierce.   How encouraging the thought, that Jesus
seeks His people at their worst, and has a perfect
control over them and their adversaries.   He did
not simply look at this poor man at a distance,
but went to where he was; and thus, by His
Word, and Spirit, He visits His people now.   Did
He wait for a lucid interval, they would never be
saved.

"*But when he saw Jesus afar off,* he ran and
worshipped him, and cried with a loud voice, and
said, What have I to do with thee, Jesus, thou Son
of the most high God?   I adjure thee by God,
that thou torment me not."

He ran towards Jesus.   The servants of Satan
knew their Master, though in the distance.   Their
faith was strong, for they had already felt the

weight of His foot and the power of His arm.
He whose omnific word hurled them from the
battlements of heaven, and but recently conquered
their king in the wilderness, was no stranger to
them. The man *ran* towards a Friend this time;
what a mercy, were it ever the case with the slaves
of Satan! But Jesus came towards him first;
and the sound of this poor man's steps were but
the echo of Christ's seeking to save His own,
though led captive of hell. The movement of
Jesus produced this. The sinner is sought, and
then he comes to his Lord. Grace takes the lead,
or who would be saved? " *I adjure thee by God;*"
Jesus is a torment to the devil; He puts but a
finger upon him, and he shrieks. What will he
feel by-and-by, when the full weight of His hand
falls upon his neck, and His fingers shall rivet
eternally the bars of his cell? " *That thou torment
me not.*" How anxious is ignorance to be cursed;
and what strange mistakes does sin put into the
heart, and bring from the lips. The poor man
expected torture from the lips of Him who came
to bring him release. Satanic influence puts forth
strange prayers. Poor Gadarene! Jesus will not
torment thee, but thy foes. The presence of
Jesus ever spoils His adversaries, and they dread
His approach. The very abysses of hell tremble
at the word of the despised Nazarene. Amid the
darkness of that dreadful pit, His eye flashes fire
as He reads the secret thoughts of the damned.

8

O'er the surging billows of eternal torment He walks, while legions of the lost gather together in groups and tremble as He passes by. In Him they see but the face of a Judge, and not a Saviour. Those who had taken possession of the Gadarene knew they had usurped His place, and would deprecate His wrath. Jesus brings terror to the ungodly, for they know He hates their sins, and has forbidden the pleasures they love; hence they ignore His authority, and deem His yoke a torment and a grief. Men would not be exorcised of their sins, though the pit of hell were their doom. Dreadful infatuation! Sinner, if Jesus is not the destruction of thy sins here, He will torment thy soul hereafter.

" *For he said unto him, Come out of the man, thou unclean spirit.*" Surely these words should have been received with joy; but how unwilling is man to be blessed. The hand that would loosen his bonds he spurns aside. In love with the sins which have mastered him, he deems it torment to be delivered from them, and hates the efforts of those who would snatch him from his doom. But Jesus heeded not the ravings of the demoniac,— He knew who dictated his prayer. He will spoil the works of the devil, without asking the permission of his slaves. And observe how potent is His word. Hell comes weeping to his feet: " And he *besought*," &c. (verses 10, 11, 12.) The devils were united in their prayer: they preferred the swine to their native pit. "Oh, send us not to it," said they; "turn not the bolts and bars of that dread prison-house upon us before our time; hurl us not into that sea of wrath. We know Thou art the Son of God; we know Thy voice, and have felt Thy power before—that Thou hast the keys of David—that the door of our prison swings backwards and forwards at Thy command. Oh, permit us to go at large for at least a little time longer."

"*And forthwith Jesus gave them leave*," &c. The swine were His property, and it was more important that His power should be displayed, than that they should be preserved,—that the demoniac should be delivered, than that they should live. He "*gave them leave.*" He did not command them, but left them simply to take their own course. He granted their request. "Oh," say some, "we are too sinful to pray, too depraved for Christ to answer us." What, are you worse than these devils? They cried, and Jesus answered them; and will He not answer those who plead His own words? But will not the conduct of these devils condemn the prayerless one? They had no promise to plead, yet they prayed; thou hast many, but thy voice is never heard.

Thus, then, the incurable was cured, and the demoniac of the tombs became a trophy of Divine power and an epistle of Divine love. The deliverance was miraculous, and it was free; and

how free is that grace which brings us from the
bondage of Satan and the slavery of sin! It was
complete also,—the entire legion was driven out
of the man; and Jesus will carry on His work
until sin is completely destroyed in His people;
and the period will come when He who saved the
poor Gadarene from his foes, will loosen us finally
and for ever from the bonds of mortality and sin,
to gather us around His throne, to serve Him
without molestation for ever.

And the poor Gadarene, that was so delivered,
was beheld sitting at the feet of Jesus, "*clothed
and in his right mind.*" The mercy of Jesus is
the only medicine of the soul. When He heals
the conscience, He enlightens the mind. The
Gadarene came to himself when he came to Jesus.
A right mind brought him to a right place—to
sit in humility and love at the feet of his Saviour.
And when Jesus forgives a man his sins, he will
ever take the lowest place, while his chief anxiety
will be to put the crown upon the head of his re-
deeming Lord.

And He who gave mental vigour to the demoniac's mind, gave decent clothing to his back;
and when Jesus pardons the soul, He clothes it
with righteousness—a righteousness which His
own hands have wrought, which outshines the
heavens in their brightness, and which shall never
decay. And when this transpires, "the lame
man leaps as the hart, while the tongue of the

dumb is made to sing;" the heart is made glad,
while the lips exclaim, with the church of old,
" I will greatly rejoice in the Lord, my soul shall
be joyful in my God; for he hath clothed me
with the garments of salvation, he hath covered
me with the robe of righteousness, as a bridegroom decketh himself with ornaments, and as a
bride adorneth herself with her jewels."

How dignified was the position, now, of the despised demoniac. O favoured Gadarene! brought
from thy dwelling among the tombs to the feet
of Jesus—from frenzy and despair, to reason,
happiness, and peace! Thy soul, once a chamber
of devils, now a temple for God, the home of His
Spirit, and the throne of His Son; once a lodge
of desolation, now a palace of joy; once a waste
howling wilderness, now a very Carmel of fruitfulness and joy! And when the redeemed shall
have reached the presence of Jesus above, all
clothed in their spotless robes, and all their mental powers attuned to the harmonies of heaven,
freed for ever from the guilt and frenzy of sin,
oh, what a picture of purity and joy will appear
for ever, to mirror forth the love of God's heart!
And when those so favoured, looking down from
the heights of glory to the regions of death they
once inhabited, the city of tombs in which they
once dwelt; and where, clothed in the raiment
of corruption and habiliments of sorrow and
shame, like the poor Gadarene, they once wan-

8*

dered, the very pictures of ruin and vocal epi-
taphs of despair, how will the song of grateful
adoration for ever ascend to Him who cast off
the shining robes of glory, and forsook the realms
of light, to visit and to save them from themselves and their foes; to transform them from the
frenzied maniacs of sin, and demons of darkness,
into children of light and heirs of a blissful immortality.   To lift them from a moral charnel-
house, and the gates of perdition, to a mansion of
glory and the presence of the King of kings and
Lord of lords.

" *And when he was come into the ship, he that had
been possessed with the devil prayed him that he might
be with him.*"

The wounded patient desires to keep near to
the friendly hand which binds up his wounds.
The timid lamb, which has been exposed to the
storm, loves to nestle in the shepherd's bosom,
where it found shelter from the blast.   The heart
that has been wounded by sin seeks to keep near
to the physician who heals; and he who has
passed through the deep waters of soul tribulation,
would ever abide with Him whose Almighty hand
plucked him from its waves.

" *And he departed, and began to publish in Deca-
polis how great things Jesus had done for him: and
all men did marvel.*"   And who can wonder at
this? had he remained silent the very stones of
the streets would have cried out against him.

And who better qualified to preach than he? He had been in Satan's service, and could expose his tyranny :—he could not only speak of his chains, but show the scars in his flesh;—his wounds would give force to his language, and make his words understood. His lips have poured forth blasphemies; they shall now utter truth; Hell had made his voice the organ of despair; Jesus will make it the trumpet of his fame, through which he will proclaim liberty to the captive and the discomfiture of Satan. His savage yells have alarmed and annoyed many; but Christ has selected that bruised reed, and the Spirit of God will now breathe through it strains of sweetest music. And this is the way that Jesus makes all his preachers. He sends them not to make known their own inventions, nor to proclaim human systems, but to tell what he has done for them. The heart must teach the lip, if the Word is to fall with power: real eloquence has its basis in sincerity, and gathers its arguments from love.

This poor Gadarene wandered among the tombs, and was the sport of Satan; but still he was a man, and Jesus visited him; and hence we may gather lessons from his life. Let us never despise the worst of our fellow-creatures, much less treat them with contempt and scorn.

Let us remember we are all implicated in the same condemnation, and that if we have not gone to the same lengths of sin, or been mastered by precisely the same spiritual adversaries, we *have* all been enslaved, and thus we should have continued but for the grace of him who liberated the poor Gadarene. And let us imitate this poor man, who not only sat at the feet of his great Deliverer in faith, humility, and love, to learn more of His grace, but went forth to publish His fame. Oh, who should make known the power of Jesus, but those whom he has freed? Who should speak of His mercy, but those whose wounds it has healed? Who should exalt His love, but those who have tasted its sweetness? or magnify His grace, but those who have proved its efficacy to sanctify and save? And seeing that it is more than equal to the wants and woes of the worst, let us aim to make it known to the worst, and let it be our delight and joy to imitate our Lord, and proclaim liberty to the captive and the opening of the prison to the bound.

Does this meet the eye of one who has found the service of sin to be hard and the yoke of Satan to be heavy; who has tried to break asunder the chains by which bound, again and again, but has failed; whose efforts have only seemed to add to their weight, and who has settled down in despair, giving up all for lost. Give up all for lost, while He lives whose word drove out a legion of devils from the soul of the poor Gadarene! Give up all for lost while He lives who heard even the prayer of devils; who saved the dying thief, even at the last hour, and who has said that all who seek shall find! What madness is this! Why, thou hast been mad so to yield to sin as to become thus bound; mad thus to cut and wound thyself; but thy despair—this is the crowning act of thy madness. There *is* a hand that can loosen thee, a voice that can free thee, mercy that can heal thee, blood that can cleanse thee, a robe which can clothe thee, grace which can renew thee, a present, living and Almighty Friend that can save thee. Thou knowest his name—Jesus, the Sinner's Friend. Cease thy own labours then, and look to Him. Go to Him again and again; though thou fallest seven times a-day still go—still cry, cease not—plead His merits, hide not thy sins nor thy fears; and be assured that in the end He will come forth to thy deliverance and joy.

> "Desponding soul,
> Thy grief control,
> One true Friend is near thee;
> Thy heart may ache,
> Yet comfort take,
> Jesus will not leave thee.

> He knows thy fears—
> He counts thy tears—
> 'He riseth at thy sigh;'
> And from above
> His look of love
> Meets thine uplifted eye.

LESSONS FROM JESUS.

Thy sorrows great
He will abate;
Not long does He contend:
Let patient faith
Rest where He saith,
'There surely is an end.'

'The Lord with you,'
Thy foes pursue,
'Go forth in this thy might:'
Thy own strength small,
Yet they shall fall,
Or make a speedy flight.

Now grasp thy shield,
And never yield,
Thou wounded, weary saint;
God cannot lie—
Oh, to Him fly,
And thou shalt never faint."

H. W.

"Hope, O ye broken hearts, at last!
    The King comes on in might!
He loved us in the ages past,
    When we sat wrapp'd in night.
    Now are our sorrows o'er,
And fear and wrath to joy give place,
Since God hath made us in His grace,
    His children evermore.

O rich the gifts thou bring'st to us,
    Thyself made poor and weak;
O love beyond compare that thus
    Can foes and sinners seek!
    For this to Thee alone
We raise on high a gladsome voice,
And evermore with thanks rejoice,
    Before Thy glorious throne."

Rist.

"How wonderful the counsels of thy power!
How excellent Thy working!   How divine
That energy, which will ere long conform
All thine to Thee!   Omnipotently raise
Meanness to beauty: helplessness to strength:
Dishonour to the splendour of Thy throne :
And destitution to the wealth of heaven."

Shephard.

The Captive Loosened;

OR,

HOPE FOR THE BOUND.

" Woman, thou art loosed from thine infirmity."—Luke xiii. 12.

THERE are many things in this sad world which make the heart of man to stoop, tinge his head with grey, and cause his body prematurely to bend towards that kindred earth, where, sooner or later, he must find for a time his last home. To the many evils which sin has entailed upon man, and by which he is frequently oppressed, must also be added those which are brought upon him through the influence of Satanic agency. Of that influence, as exerted upon the body at least, we hear but little in these modern times. That our Saviour may have gathered in some few links of Apollyon's chain, in this particular, is not improbable; but that he *had* power, in by-gone ages grievously to afflict the body, as well as the mind, is abundantly evident from the Gospel narrative.

9

The evangelist Luke brings before us a woman whom a "spirit of infirmity" had bound for many years; and the Great Teacher tells us that Satanic agency was the source of her disease—that the same hand which ravished the temple of man's soul at the beginning, and robbed it of all its celestial furniture, with infernal malice, had so maltreated the frail tenement in which she dwelt, that for eighteen years she had never stood 'erect. During all these years had the great Adversary been tightening his cords about her, and frequently, no doubt, under the influence of that spirit of cruelty which ever lives in his heart, rejoiced at the thought that he should hold her body in misery to the end of her days. Of the intensity of diabolical hate we can scarcely form an adequate idea; but who can doubt its existence in the mind of him who felt a malicious delight in the fearful agonies of the Son of God? His meat and his drink is to oppose the Almighty, while the sufferings of God's creatures ever add additional relish to his infernal repast. Misery into the heart of Christ he cannot now introduce, or he would. But as he cannot reach the Master, he will, if possible, wound Him through those who love and obey Him. Could he accomplish his will, he would fill God's creation to overflowing with the same hatred, bitterness, and despair, which dwell in himself without diminution or vent.

This being the temper of man's great foe, the

sight of this "daughter of Abraham," whom he had smitten, were music to his ears, while her tears had been his solace, as he gazed upon her tottering steps and drooping form. He had seen her brow furrowed with care, and marked her fruitless attempts to break his bonds. She, poor creature, had often thought the hour seemed long, and with her the days rolled wearily away. Into the bosom of paternal love she had often poured out her grief; and, like Paul, besought the Lord many times to remove "the thorn" from the flesh. Again, and again, had she cried to the Lord for that help which she could not find in herself or her friends; and which all the skill of this world failed to bring. But the answer was delayed; the cloud still hung upon her path, and her foe revelled in her grief. The summer came, and the earth rejoiced in its fresh mantle of beauty; the birds sang with joy, and all around her appeared happy; but her burden remained: the summer departed, and in the lap of winter nature slept to regain her strength; but her body remained weak. The sun gilded her path by day, and the stars smiled upon her by night, but she could not look up. Her neighbours tripped gaily along, and the sons of Belial walked proudly erect by her side, and some-times, it may be, she *did* think it hard that the God of her fathers appeared to shut out her prayers, and her body still pressed towards the earth.

But the day of her deliverance came. "*And*

when Jesus saw her;" what, had He not seen her before? Yes, doubtless, her history was well known to Him. *"Behold, these eighteen years she hath been bound,"* said he; while these years passed tediously along, she could scarcely help thinking that her sorrows were entirely overlooked; but the days of her affliction were numbered, and the time appointed when they should cease had now arrived. He who counted the stars will not be too late, either to confound her adversary, or loosen her bonds. Satan had not had the house entirely to himself. Could he have pulled down its walls he would have done so with fiendish glee; but Christ held them up. She was a *"daughter of Abraham,"* and that stooping and oft weary body was His temple; He knew the place well, and it had long been determined that Satan's cruel work should all be undone.

And now the eye of Christ is upon her; yes, He looks upon the poor, and despises not the weak. *" He saw her;"* did her beauty attract Him? Alas, no: she was deformed and bound. Still He looked upon her, and mercy beams from His eye, while love moves His heart. O favoured woman, to excite the attention of Him whom angels obey; to command His regard, whose favour is life. Upon her deformed body the curious had often gazed, and ignorant mirth had sometimes pointed the finger of scorn; the wise had pondered the *cause* of her infirmity, and the benevolent expressed a passing regret. But now ONE sees her who will not only look, but help; not only speak, but cure; —" *Woman, thou art loosed from thine infirmity!*" Oh, what a surprise, what a deliverance was this! How unexpected, how free! Her only merit was disease, but one word brings her cure. She now stands erect, and her lips pour forth praise. Oh, how easily the sinner conquers when Jesus gives him strength! while he struggles alone with his sin, how vain his efforts to rise; but when Christ speaks the word, the conscience goes free; then faith finds a refuge, and Christ makes a friend. O sinner, would'st thou be free? take thy bonds to Christ; look to His blood for thy pardon, and to His grace to subdue all thy sins.

The woman is free, and He who has released her body has loosened her tongue. And will *she* praise *a man?* "*And she glorified GOD!*" Who but God could have loosed her? And can she be silent? All her movements are vocal—every step utters praise. The broken harp is retuned, all its strings are awake, and in the man who has healed her, she finds the God whom she adores. On that once infirm body Christ has now written His name, and men while they read it, shall exclaim, "This is the Lord's doing!" O Satan, thine eighteen years' labour has glorified Christ! was this thine intention? Where once thy malice was seen, now the grace of the Lord: will this serve thy cause? Men now see thou art cruel, and Jesus is love;

9*

that thou art weak, and Jesus is strong; that thou art foolish and Jesus is wise. A weak woman is thy master, and what can'st thou say? Thou did'st pull down her body—it now pulls down thee; through her weakness thou did'st wound her —her weakness now wounds thee; her frail body shall bruise thee—the body thou did'st bruise. See the woman walks erect! Try, now, can'st thou make her stoop? Come, now, scheme, labour, toil—speak! Ah, 'tis vain! mercy has lifted her up to proclaim thy defeat, and to exhibit His power, which thou art ever seeking to hide. Thus the Captain of Salvation spoils the works of the devil, plucks from his hands the heralds of his fame, and makes his malice but the foil of His love.

Let us rejoice in these truths; but let us not forget that we have drooping souls now, who stoop by the way, and who in bondage through fear, can scarcely look up; who feel their bonds, and sigh for relief; who carry their chains, and cannot get free. Let us point such to Christ; let us speak of His blood; let us tell them of His grace, and of His power to save. Has Christ made us free? Has His love melted our chains? And shall we be silent among the captives of hell? God forbid! may all our movements declare, all our words loudly proclaim, that Christ has redeemed us, and lives to loosen the bound. Can we expect to enjoy Christ if we serve not His cause? Why passes

the church homewards through the world's high-
way so frequently like a decrepit woman whom
Satan has bound? Because she lives so much to
herself, and so little to her Lord; looks so much
at her burdens, and so seldom to Him. And what
must arouse her, and quicken her movements onwards and upwards? The voice of her Beloved.
And how is she to hear it? Through the Gospel
of His grace, and the breath of His Spirit. Then
let us cleave to the former, and pray for the latter;
and let us anticipate the period, when the voice of
Christ again shall be heard, and when, spreading
His hands over the dust of His sleeping Church,
she shall arise, and standing upon the shining
summit of everlasting day, shall no longer appear
like a stooping woman whom Satan has bound,
but like a youthful bride adorned for her husband,
to exhibit His glory and laud His name.

" Thou who breakest every chain,
　　Thou who still art ever near,
　Thou with whom disgrace and pain,
　　Turn to joy and heaven, e'en here;
　Let thy further judgments fall
　　On the Adam strong within,
　Till Thy grace hath freed us all
　　From the prison house of sin.

'Tis Thy Father's will toward us,
　　Thou should'st end Thy work at length;
　Hence in thee are centred thus,
　　Perfect wisdom, love, and strength,

That Thou none should'st lose of those
   Whom He gave Thee, though they roam
'Wilder'd here amid their foes,
   Thou should'st bring them safely home.

Ah, Thou wilt, Thou can'st not cease,
   Till Thy perfect work be done;
In Thy hands we lie at peace,
   Knowing all Thy love hath won.
Though the world may blindly dream
   We are captives, poor and base,
And the cross's yoke may deem
   Sign of meanness and disgrace.

Look upon our bonds, and see
   How doth all creation groan
'Neath the yoke of vanity;
   Make Thy full redemption known;
Still we wrestle, cry, and pray;
   Held in bitter bondage fast,
Though the soul would break away
   Into higher things at last.

Lord we do not ask for rest
   For the flesh; we only pray
Thou would'st do as seems Thee best,
   Ere yet comes our parting day;
But our Spirit clings to Thee;
   Will not, dare not, let Thee go,
Until Thou have set her free
   From the bonds that cause her woe.

Ruler come, and Conqueror conquer;
   King assert Thy sovereign right,
Till there be no slavery longer.
   Spread the kingdom of Thy might!

Lead the captive freely out,
  Through the covenant of Thy blood,
From our dark remorse and doubt,
  For Thou wilt alone our good.

'Tis of our own fault we own;
  We are slaves to self and sloth;
Yet, oh, leave us not alone
  In the living death we loathe!
Crush'd beneath our burden's weight,
  Crying at Thy feet we fall;
Point the path, though steep and straight,
  Thou did'st open once for all.

Ah! how dearly were we bought,
  Not to serve the world or sin;
By the work that Thou hast wrought
  Must Thou make us pure within,—
Wholly pure and free, in us
  Be thine image now restored:
Fill'd from out Thy fulness thus
  Grace for grace is on us pour'd.

Draw us to Thy cross; O Love,
  Crucify with Thee whate'er
Cannot dwell with Thee above,
  Lead us to those regions fair!
Courage! long the time may seem,
  Yet His day is coming fast;
We shall be like them that dream,
  When our freedom dawns at last."

GOTTFRIED ARNOLD, 1697.
Lyra Germanica.

"O Father-eye, that hath so truly watched,
  O Father-hand, that hath so gently led,
O Father-heart, that by my prayer is touched,
    That loved me first when I was cold and dead:
Still do Thou lead me on with faithful care
    The narrow path to heaven, where I would go,
And train me for the life that waits me there,
    Alike through love and loss, through weal and woe."

SPITTA.

"It is a sign some beam of heavenly wisdom hath shined into that soul, which findeth itself empty of true saving wisdom."— John xvi. 8, 9. 2 Cor. iv. 6.

BAIN.

Jesus and the Blind Man;

OR,

A GUIDE FOR THE PERPLEXED.

" And he took the blind man by the hand, and led him out of the town."—Mark viii. 23.

As the lover of art, when passing through those galleries which are filled with the works of the great masters, frequently has his attention excited and his admiration called forth by the discovery of some new beauty springing forth from that force and freshness which ever mark the productions of genius, so the believer, as in meditation he passes through the gallery of Divine Revelation, frequently meets with pictures so full of grace, and pregnant with spiritual instruction, that with the poet he is compelled to exclaim :—

> " Father of mercies! in Thy word
> What endless glory shines!
> For ever be Thy name adored,
> For these celestial lines."

Among the choicest gems of the Cabinet of Truth, perhaps none is more attractive than that presented by the divine historian above,—Jesus leading the blind man forth from the town of Bethsaida.

How marvellous the grouping; how striking the contrast! Here we see mercy and misery, darkness and light, health and disease, omnipotence and frailty, locked hand in hand, and walking through the streets together. Hundreds of years before, this interesting scene had filled the prophetic eye of the seraphic Isaiah, when he wrote thus of the Shiloh of his people: "He shall lead the blind by a way that they know not, and in paths which they have not known." There we have the seed, here the flower in full bloom; there the prophetic sketch, here the picture completed and filled in by the hand of the Master Himself; and should it not be prized by us, especially as it so richly portrays His dealings with ourselves? Believing that the life of Christ illustrated His doctrine, and not only embodies the substance of His teaching, but is its most vivid exponent, let us look at our Lord as He traverses the streets of Bethsaida. May the Holy Spirit instruct us, as we follow Him in His pilgrimage of mercy, and may our hearts be deeply affected by our contemplations.

"*And he took the blind man by the hand.*" Let us look at this poor man awhile; he claimed the attention of Christ, why should He not have ours; he cannot see, but he may exhibit ourselves. He is in the midst of the town, and surrounded with objects, but he sees them not. Art may exhibit her stores, and Nature her charms, but they affect him not. Spring throws her flowers beneath his feet, Summer spreads her varied glories, and Autumn her richest tints, but he heeds them not; all around him rejoices with an exuberance of joy, but he rejoices not. The sun falls upon his path, but nature is ever clothed in sackcloth to him; the ebon curtains of a perpetual night enfold him in their embrace without one solitary star to relieve the gloom. He sleeps, but it is night; he awakes, but there is no morning. Sad condition : still sadder that of which it is but a faint type : " *Ye were darkness*," says the Apostle ; not *in* the dark, but darkness. We were in the midst of light, but it reached not the mind; the cataract of sin permitted no single ray to pass; and so deep was the darkness, that though we stood in the midst of this fair creation, yet we perceived not its great Author, or, if we perceived Him, our language was, " *Depart from us, for we desire not the knowledge of thy ways.*" We sometimes, too, went into the field of Divine Revelation, but beheld not its chief glory ; or, when our eye fell upon Him to whom all the prophets gave witness, we declared Him to be " a root out of a dry

10

ground, having no form nor comeliness that we should desire him."

Of this poor blind man we observe: *He was exposed to great danger,*—he was in the midst of a town, liable at any moment to be injured or destroyed. And how great is our danger as blinded by sin ;—foes within us and foes without us, yet insensible to our condition ; encompassed by the snares of Hell, exposed to the curse of God, and liable at any moment to be struck down by death, and hurried to the bar of God.

He was past human help. His friends took him to Jesus ; they had, no doubt, exhausted all their skill, and this was their last resource. Possibly they belonged to the *literati* of their country; were educated and polite, philosophical as well as kind, but they could not restore his sight, they could not give eyes to the blind. And who can break in upon the gloom and darkness of the sin-imprisoned mind; who can cast into its deep recesses that vivid ray which dispels the dark night of prejudice, ignorance, and enmity so that Jesus is seen as He is ? Philosophy here is foiled ; education labours in vain ; science and art pour forth their gentle, humanising radiance in vain; clothed in more than Cimmerian darkness, the soul still toils on in the midst of its desolation, and God still remains unloved, because unknown. " God who commandeth the light to shine out of darkness, must shine into our hearts to *give* us the light

of the knowledge of the glory of God in the face
of Jesus Christ."

"*He took him by the hand.*" Did He forget He
was the Son of God? Oh, no! nor was it needful he should; for never are the great so exalted
as when they stoop to the help of misery, and
endeavour to raise those who but for their aid
must be for ever fallen. He was not ashamed to
do good, or too great to be useful. Are we
ashamed to grasp the hand of honest poverty, or
to be seen identified with misery? If so, let us
not call ourselves the disciples of Him who led
the blind man through the town of Bethsaida;
but let us seek to have this scene painted upon
the walls of our memory, and engraven upon our
hearts, until, constrained by the love of Jesus,
and following His example, we are declared to be
one in spirit with Him who said, "If any man
will be my disciple, let him deny himself, and
take up his cross and follow me."

"*He took him by the hand.*" He was sufficiently
familiar to be useful. "Oh," say the rich, "we
wish we could serve the poor;" then do not visit
them in state: say the educated, "We desire to
instruct the ignorant;" then address them in
their own language.

"*Jesus took him by the hand.*" He did not say,
"Do you take hold of my hand," or " Keep by my
side, and I will conduct you out of the city."
No; but "*He took him by the hand.*" Neither

does Jesus say to the dark, the guilty, and the self-condemned, "Now, do you do such and such things, and then I will help you; get you so much light, and then I will shine upon you; make yourselves so far righteous, and I will supply that which you lack." No; but He shines upon the soul freely, reveals His glory, and *gives* faith to the soul, while he exclaims, "Believe, and live."

"*He took him by the hand.*" Yes, though the blind man saw Him not, and knew not the character of Him who led him through the town. And what knew we of Jesus when He first visited us? Little thought we that the truths which so deeply affected our minds at first, and from the influence of which we could not escape, were but the omnipotent fingers of Jesus, grasping our immortal spirits, and seeking to draw us to Himself. Had He consulted us ere He thus led us, we should, it may be, have repelled His advances; but He drew us with the cords of love and the bands of a man, and thus fulfilled his own declaration: "I taught Ephraim also to go, leading them by their arms; and they knew not that I healed them."

"*He led him.*" The blind man was willing to be led—most blind men are; and when men are conscious of their own ignorance and liability to err, to mistake the way which leads to heaven, they are glad to take Christ for their guide.

While men vainly deem their own wit and wisdom sufficient to conduct them safely through the
mazes of life, and to the home of the blest, they
will never seek the direction of Him who has
promised "to guide His people with His eye, and
to counsel them in the way they should go."

"*He* LED *him.*" He did not forget He was
leading a blind man, and accommodated His pace
to the condition of His patient. Had he moved
too quickly, the man might have fallen. Some are
too quick of understanding to be of much service
to others; their minds move too rapidly for the
multitude · to follow them. Observe yonder
young man in the city of error; he is bewildered
and astonished with its numberless streets and
multitudinous turnings—some this way and some
that. A palace now attracts his attention;
"What a magnificent pile of architecture!" he
exclaims. "Nonsense!" replies a person hastily
passing by; and seeking to drag him after him,
as he hurries on. "What, admire that?" "Yes,
I do," exclaims the young man, resisting the
attempt to move him; "I never saw a building
more worthy of admiration." Another person
arrives, like unto Him who led the blind man
through the town of Bethsaida, and, gently taking
him by the hand, kindly asks him to accompany
Him into the interior; and, as they gaze upon
the inmates, the young man grasps the hand of
his guide more closely, and follows Him slowly
10*

to other parts of the town. From the gay thoroughfares and brilliant streets, he is led into the dark alleys and squalid courts. Still more tightly does he grasp the friendly hand which guides him, until at last, and step by step, he is conducted beyond the precincts of that which he once deemed to be an illustrious city. Is not the moral plain? Through how many mental mazes, streets of error, and dark alleys of moral death, has not Jesus guided our often faltering and undecided feet, nor left us until brought safely into the field of revealed truth, and clear sunshine of divine favour? How has He cleared up our skies again and again; removed our perplexities, and said to us, " *This is the way, walk ye in it?*" When we could not see our way either to pardon or peace, how kindly did He show it. He took us by the hand when no one else did, or could; when we must have perished, he came to our rescue. "When no eye did pity, and when no arm could save, then it was that His eye pitied and His arm saved."

> " Oh for such love let rocks and hills
> Their lasting silence break;
> And all harmonious human tongues
> The Saviour's praises speak!"

" *He led him out of the town.*" Jesus always leads *from* danger. Oh, what numberless dangers we should escape if we were always willing for Him to lead us!

"*Out of the town.*" He meant to cure him; but He did not want fame—the applause of the multitude. His object was simply to open his eyes; hence he conducted him into privacy. Be assured of this, dear reader, that if Jesus opens the eyes of your mind, he will draw you away *from* the world.

"*And when he had spit on his eyes, and put his hands upon him, he asked him if he saw aught.*" Very unlikely instrumentality, many would have thought, to open the eyes; but thus it is that Jesus is pleased to work, that He may have the glory due to His name, for God hath chosen "the foolish things of the world to confound the wise, and God hath chosen the weak things of the world to confound the things which are mighty; and base things of the world, and things which are despised, hath God chosen; yea, and things which are not, to bring to nought things that are."

"*And he looked up.*" Whenever Jesus savingly enlightens the mind, the character is sure to be elevated. No matter how debased we may have been, our affections will no longer cleave to the earth. It will no longer be true of us that we resemble him of whom it is written, that when in heaven his eyes were fixed more upon its golden pavement than upon Him who sat on the throne.

"*And he said, I see men as trees, walking.*" A

misty morning has frequently ushered in a glorious day; and as in nature, so in grace. Where light from Jesus breaks in upon us, we see many objects, but none clearly; let not, therefore, the perplexed seeker after truth be discouraged, but wait upon the Lord, who will ever bring His own work to a happy completion.

"*After that he put his hands again upon his eyes.*" What a mercy Jesus puts His hands upon our eyes again and again, and does not despise us on account of our ignorance and slowness to learn! He could have opened the poor man's eyes *at once* had it pleased Him, but He did not; and He could bring all His people into the light and liberty of the Gospel at once were it His will to do so; but He is pleased rather to lead many of them progressively, step by step, teaching them here a little, and there a little, as they are able to bear it. Let us praise Him for His grace, and take heed of limiting the operations of His Spirit.

"*And he was restored, and saw every man clearly.*" He who begins a good work in us will carry it on until it is perfected above. However dubious our perceptions of the truth may be at first, if we are willing and anxious to be taught, Jesus will scatter our darkness, nor leave us until our hearts are established in those truths which are essential to our safety and peace. "*The path of the just is as the morning light, which increaseth unto the perfect day.*"

Perhaps some who have perused these thoughts may be much distressed in reference to their path. Be encouraged, dear reader, to trust your way in the hands of Him who led the poor blind man through the town of Bethsaida; or is the reader perplexed as to what is the truth? If so, seek the teaching of Him who opened the blind man's eyes, and He will guide you to establishment and rest.

Are we troubled by those whom we have often sought to lead in the right way, but in vain, and who seem intent on their own destruction? Let us take them to Him who took the blind man by the hand, and who is able to preserve them from the dangers which surround them. Are we conscious that the Lord has opened our eyes? What humility and gratitude become us! How unseemly it would have been for the blind man to *boast* of his sight. How offensive to the Lord must spiritual pride be in those who are indebted to Him for both their knowledge and faith. Let us cultivate deep self-abasement of spirit, and strive to imitate Jesus in seeking to lead the ignorant from danger to the paths of purity and peace.

Does the reader imagine he has sufficient wisdom to guide himself safely through life, and even to the kingdom of glory above? Hear the word of God: "It is *not* in man to direct his steps." The fact that God has promised to guide His people with His eye, is sufficient to prove that they cannot guide themselves. Be assured of this,

dear reader, that if you do not seek the guidance
of Him, who in the days of His flesh, took the
blind man by the hand to lead him from the town
of Bethsaida, Satan, his great adversary, will
ensnare your soul, and finally drag you down to
eternal perdition.   Wilt thou not, therefore, from
this time cry to the Lord, and say, "My Father,
be thou the guide of my youth?"

"O Christ, our true and only light,
Illumine those who sit in night;
Let those afar now hear Thy voice,
And in Thy fold with us rejoice.

Fill with the radiance of Thy grace,
The souls now lost in error's maze,
And all whom in their secret minds
Some dark delusion hurts and blinds.

And all who else have strayed from Thee,
Oh gently seek! Thy healing be
To every wounded conscience given,
And let them also share Thy heaven.

Oh make the deaf to hear Thy word,
And teach the dumb to speak, dear Lord,
Who dare not yet the faith avow,
Though secretly they hold it now.

Shine on the darkened and the cold,
Recall the wanderers from Thy fold,
Unite those now who walk apart,
Confirm the weak and doubting heart;

So they with us may evermore
Such grace with wondering thanks adore,
And endless praise to Thee be given
By all Thy church in earth and heaven."

J. HEERMAN.   1630.

Lyra Germanica.

"Let those that sow in sadness wait
Till the fair harvest come!
They shall confess their sheaves are great,
And shout the blessings home.

The seed, though buried long in dust,
Shall not deceive their hope:
The precious grain can ne'er be lost,
For grace ensures the crop."

"Observe, *that God conveys truths into the hearts of His people unawares.* As they often expect and wait long for knowledge, so they sometimes know before they expect. A truth, either in whole or in part, in the matter or clearer light of it, comes like a *thief* into the heart, *suddenly, secretly,* unlooked for: in which case it is ever true, *that truth unexpected is doubly welcomed.* The way of the Spirit of God is always undiscernible to flesh and blood. The soul receives a thing, and the man knows not how; he can (scarce possibly, not at all) tell where, by whom, or which way it came to him; it was brought, and with a most blessed, *gracious sleight of hand, conveyed into his heart.* Yet sometimes truth enters *in state;* and it may be said to make its passage visibly, into the heart of the man. The word comes not as a company of thieves, but as a band of soldiers, with weapons drawn, and terrible shouts, tearing open the soul and breaking open the iron gate of the heart, locked and barred by unbelief, to secure that cursed crew of lusts garrisoned within it. The weapons of our warfare (saith the apostle) are mighty through God; the word is mighty, wonderful in strength; it comes upon the soul as an armed man, to spoil it of all sinful treasures, yea, of the very life of sin. Sometimes the Lord proclaims war, as by an herald of arms against a man, and openly prepares for his siege and battery. *He surprises another, and steals him into a happy captivity to Himself.*"—CARYL.

Jesus and the Growing Corn;

OR,

THE PROGRESS OF DIVINE LIFE.

"For the earth bringeth forth fruit of herself; first the blade, then the ear, after that the full corn in the ear."— Mark iv. 28.

THIS world is a pregnant symbol of divine things —a vast temple full of sublime and beautiful forms, all of which point to something beyond themselves. It is a book upon which God has written His name, in varied characters it is true, but plain enough to all who wish to read it. And as we descend below the surface of the earth we turn over many leaves, all of which are instructive; though it may still be affirmed that this book, like another of which we read, is comparatively a sealed book. We have seen but a few of its pages; the table of its contents who can bring before us, or when will it be fully read? A glorious and gifted man, too, but recently de-

11

parted, has pointed us to the "testimony of the
rocks." Yes, and they speak well, and eloquently
too, for God and truth. Men viewed them as
dry and barren things. Not so; instinct with
life, they have a voice for God. Men would have
made them fight against their Maker, and have
forced their pointed summits through the heart
of Truth; but they could not, for even now she
lives, and laughs, and claps her hands upon the
rocks. "See here," she says, pointing to them;
"behold God's cabinet, in which His wisdom has
sealed up the most ancient records of this world's
history, and all confirmatory of the sacred page.
I speak, and Nature speaks; we both agree."
We turn to these ancient records, and learn that
God has ever made use of the surface of the earth
as a tablet on which to write His name. And
while this planet at various periods has presented
many such tablets to the sun, none of them were
blanks; the same hand which wrote Belshazzar's
doom upon his palace walls was ever present
to incribe upon them the lines of wisdom and
of power, and intimations of a crowning design
more richly pregnant with the varied forms of
Almighty and unwearied love. Never, however,
did the earth present so bright a surface to the
sun as that on which we dwell, or so filled with
the beautiful and highly-finished illustrations of
the perfections of its great Creator. The preceding
surfaces were touched by the finger of God; the

present bears the footprints of His Son, and its dust formed part of that holy temple in which He dwelt during His weary pilgrimage below. On the preceding tablets we mark the seal of wisdom and power, while now, aided by other light than that which comes from the sun, we behold spreading around us so many pictorial representations of *grace*, and the whole of Nature's progeny blending their colours harmoniously together to paint forth the glory of that kingdom of which Christ is the centre and head. Hence we view the present surface of this planet as more honoured of God than any other which has preceded; all its varied products being brought under tribute more immediately to Christ. Its flowers form His garland, its precious stones the ornaments of His crown. There might have been other roses before, but they did not point to the Rose of Sharon; other plants, but they were not representative of "the Plant of Renown." . Instructed, therefore, by God's book, it is pleasant to contemplate the teachings of Nature, to listen to her voice; and how much rather would we listen to her sometimes than to the lords of creation, for she is not lordly. Here is a tree, really a *great* tree—how many are its branches, how numberless its leaves!—now, if we venture to speak of it, to notice or pass our opinion upon it, it will not throw its heavy branches upon us, or twist its great arms around us to drag us to the earth, much less destroy us, but it will spread its green mantle over us to screen us from the sun, yield us its fruit, and incite us to muse or speak as we please. Now, mark yon self-important theologian, whose opinions are as numberless as the leaves of this tree, but altogether destitute, however, of that sap of life which makes them green and useful; and venture a word upon the value of this leafy greatness—ah! down you go, a rotten branch; the fire must have you. Ye sons of power and peace, who would not rather talk to a tree than a man? Why, Nature, thy brambles are not so cruel as some saints; thou hast no thorns to pierce as do their words, even when our violent hands do most rudely grasp thee. We may safely wander in the fields, then. Yes, and Jesus will accompany us; and, walking with Him, they will yield us more than logic ever did, or human art, or seats of learning, so called; the flowers will teach us more than some men, while Christ bids them preach to us the life of simple faith in God. The corn-fields, too, must yield us more than temporal bread, for, said Christ, "So is the kingdom of God, as if a man should cast seed into the ground; and should sleep, and rise night and day, and the seed should spring and grow up, he knoweth not how. For the earth bringeth forth fruit of herself; first the blade, then the ear, after that the full corn in the ear." Without going very minutely into the meaning of our Saviour's language, or the specific object He had in view in uttering it, we shall make use of the figure it presents to us to illustrate the work of divine grace in the heart in its commencement, progress, and maturity.

The green blade.—How beautiful it appears in the midst of the melting snow, and after the winter's storms are hushed into quiet and repose! And how beautiful does the green blade of godly fear appear as it springs forth in the life of one whose whole life has been one continued storm of reckless pride and passion!

How beautiful does the green blade appear in the midst of the putrefaction. which frequently surrounds it! And how attractive is true religion as it springs forth and developes itself in the life and conduct of the young, who, notwithstanding that they are surrounded by all the blandishments of sense and the corruptions of a vile and apostate world, still grow up in conformity to Christ! How lovely to see such maintaining their integrity, keeping their garments white and unspotted from the world, and shedding on all around the purifying and elevating influence of their holy life!

How beautiful does the green blade appear in the midst of decay and death! And oh, how pleasant to see the green blade of faith springing forth in the prayers, tears, and godly sorrow of the aged, even in the midst of death!—to mark these wanderers even at the eleventh hour come back to that God and Saviour so long forgotten and despised. Oh, we say, thanks to God that in the midst of the winter of death the green blade of hope lifts up its head to chase away the dark cloud of despair!

How silently does the green blade come forth from the bosom of the earth—were you to place your ear close to the virgin soil, it would bring you no intelligence of the life springing up. And with what noiseless steps does divine mercy come to the sinner's heart to make way for the sinner's Friend; how gently does the hand of love remove our chains ofttimes; how softly does the dew of heaven steal into the heart to cause the seed of truth to germinate and grow.

How gradually does the green blade show itself: though the eye were fixed upon the earth both night and day, the exact moment when it appeared could not be ascertained. And who can tell the precise hour when the omnipotent finger of God's Spirit first touched the heart, the first dewdrop of heaven's mercy distilled upon the spirit? Does this perplex thee, reader? mind not the moment. Does the husbandman refuse to rejoice as he beholds the growing corn because he cannot tell the time when it pierced the sod?—and why shouldst thou distress thyself about the time when thou wast blessed? Hast thou the blade of faith—the plant of godly fear? Rejoice, the hand of God bade it take root within thy heart; let it be thy concern to have its leaves kept green by heavenly influences.

Forget not that prayer has often made the heavens drop fatness on our path, and the everlasting hills to pour their fructifying streams.

With what a mysterious yet invincible power does the green blade force its way through the heavy clods which cover it, and hide it from view! So frail is it that the slighest bruise threatens to beat it to the earth, while yet so omnipotent is it that it will spring forth to the light, however great the weight which may be cast upon it—and how strikingly this energy of vegetable life illustrates that life which is divine. The plants of righteousness, though they may be heavily weighed by a body of sin and death—by manifold sorrows, temptations, and fears—will nevertheless grow upwards towards the great Source of eternal day. Satan may place the heavy foot of persecution upon the growing kingdom of Christ, but he cannot press out its life, for its roots are divine; he may endeavour to put his finger upon the rising sap in the true vine that so the branches may not appear, but he cannot—he may cut them off, but they bud forth again. The life which Christ imparts to the soul will rise and rise until, overflowing the bounds of sinful fear and the conventionalisms of the world, it bursts into the life bearing down all opposition, and compelling even the ungodly to admit that Christ has gained another friend. Reader dost thou entertain the hope that thou hast received life from

Christ?   Take heed, examine; life will manifest
itself.   Wouldst thou prevent this; and, listening
to thy own timid heart and the suggestions of
Satan, hast thou sought to hide the expressions of
life beneath the cold, damp soil of worldly policy?
O foolish sexton! thus to bury thy hope.   What
evidence hast thou that thou hast life at all?
Hast thou not read that there is *first the blade?*
it must come forth—it will declare itself.   Art
thou not afraid?   Hast thou pondered the words
of Christ, "Whosoever, therefore, shall be ashamed
of Me, and of My words, in this adulterous and
sinful generation, of him also shall the Son of man
be ashamed, when He cometh in the glory of His
Father with the holy angels?"   Awake, arouse
thyself, and let thy love display itself in keeping
the commandments of Christ.

The green blade.—How it flourishes apparently
without human care, for "so is the kingdom of
God," said Christ, "as if a man should cast seed
in the ground; and should sleep, and rise night
and day, and the seed should spring and grow up,
he knoweth not how."   And how wise and beneficent are these arrangements.   How small would
be the quantity of bread we should have did it
depend entirely upon the husbandman's care; but
having taken a certain course with his seed, he
eats, drinks, and sleeps, and waits the issue; and
God Himself, too frequently unsolicited, and without receiving even the pepper-corn-rent of grati-

tude or praise, watches over the buried grain, and brings it to a joyful maturity in the full harvest-home. So frequently does the servant of Jesus go forth and scatter with no sparing hand the precious seed of truth; sometimes he too fails to water it as he should with his prayers and tears. The seed and the place where scattered are forgotten; and frequently, even when the green blade is seen, it is overlooked. But not so with God; He marked each golden grain of truth, and the heart opened by Himself to receive it was well known to Him; and without even the thought, care, or prayers of His servant, in many instances the work is brought to perfection. The salvation of the people He loves, redeemed by the precious blood of His Son, and destined to be His crown of rejoicing, is far too important to hang upon the faithfulness or prayers of even His most devoted servants; and who is there, however he may have laboured, watched, and prayed, who does not rejoice that it is so, and who will not with tears of gratitude, confess that while he has been all but comparatively careless, and has all but *slept*, God has carried on His own work, and saved many through efforts which we could not have dared to have thought worthy of His recognition, on account of the spirit in which they were made? But thus it is that God humbles His servants, while by His most gratuitous blessings He shows them what they are, and while thus extorting praise from their lips, demonstrates to their hearts that the salvation of those over whom they rejoice is "not of him that willeth, nor of him that run-neth, but of God that showeth mercy." And because God is thus faithful to His work, and watches over it with an unslumbering care, how frequently are His children found in most unlikely places, and growing and thriving under the most unpropitious circumstances. The Church ex-claims as of old, "Where have these been?" The secret is this; that He who watches over the little flower as it bends its head in the valley, crowning its head, morning by morning, with a coronal of dewdrops, watches over His people, and fre-quently, without any human instrumentality, per-fects His love in their hearts, and brings them to Zion: and why should those who have been thus dealt with distress themselves because they cannot tell *how* the work was accomplished. Be it suffi-cient for thee to know, dear reader, that if thou hast found thy way to the feet of Jesus, the gentle hand of God's Spirit has conducted thee,—that if thine eyes are opened to the beauties of holiness, the same hand has opened them. Leave the method with God, rejoice over the result, remem-bering who has said, "For so is the kingdom of God, as if a man should cast seed into the ground; and should sleep, and rise night and day, and the seed should spring and grow up, he *knoweth not how.*"

And after the blade comes the ear pregnant with hope. On the first appearance of the blade, its true character might have been doubted by the uneducated eye; but now the rounded bulbs at once declare its worth to man, and wherever the green blade of earnest prayer shows itself with sorrow for sin, there, sooner or later, the other Christian graces will come forth; the knowlege imparted will become clearer, the character will become consolidated, and the young man in Christ will appear strong to bear and do the will of God.

Then comes the full corn in the ear, and this, matured and ripened, meekly bending its head with the weight of its own glory, stands before us, a beautiful symbol of the aged saint, who, with his graces mellowed and matured, awaits the hand of love to gather him into the garner above.

Corn, however, to be seen to perfection, must be viewed as ripened beneath the light of the sun; and of the saint it may be said, that while in every stage of the divine life his character appears lovely, this is pre-eminently the case as it is matured and fitted for the mansions above. Still, after all, it must be affirmed that the growing corn of which Jesus speaks will never be seen in all its perfection and beauty, until it is beheld waving upon the everlasting hills, and beneath the light of that sun which shall never set.

May we be numbered among those whose character divine grace will thus perfect here, and crown with felicity hereafter.

"Sow in the morn thy seed,
    At eve hold not thy hand;
To doubt and fear give thou no heed,
    Broadcast it round the land.

Beside all waters sow,
    The highway furrows stock:
Drop it where thorns and thistles grow;
    Scatter it on the rock.

The good, the fruitful ground
    Expect not here nor there;
Air, hill, and dale, by plots 'tis found;
    Go forth, then, everywhere.

Thou know'st not which may thrive,
    The late or early sown;
Grace keeps the precious germ alive,
    When and wherever shown.

And duly shall appear,
    In verdure beauty, strength,
The tender blade, the stalk, the ear,
    And one full corn at length.

Thou canst not toil in vain;
    Cold, heat, and moist, and dry,
Shall foster and mature the grain
    For garners in the sky."

MONTGOMERY.

"Despise not thou a small thing, either for evil or good;
For a *look* may work thy ruin, or a word create thy wealth.
That which vexeth thee now, provoking thee to hate thy
    brother,
Bear with it; the annoyance passeth, and may not return for
    ever.
A little explained—a little endured—a little passed over as a
    foible,
And lo! the jagged atoms fit like smooth mosaic."

PROVERBIAL PHILOSOPHY.

"He that never changed any of his opinions, never corrected
any of his mistakes; and he who was never wise enough to find
out any mistakes in himself, will not be charitable enough to
excuse what he reckons mistakes in others."—DR. WHICHCOTE.

"Advice, like snow, the softer it falls, the longer it dwells
upon, and the deeper it sinks into the mind."—COLERIDGE.

"Trust him little who praises all, him less who censures all,
and him least who is indifferent about all."—LAVATER.

Kind Words;

OR,

A LESSON FOR THE ANGRY.

"Speaking the truth in love."—Eph. iv. 15.

LOVE is said to be an omnipotent law, and kind-ness is certainly the child of love, and partakes of the strength of its parent. The injury done by harsh words can never be properly estimated, the holy victories gained by kind words can never be properly numbered. Harsh words have stumbled many a weary traveller, and broken many a down-cast one; they carry anger to the soul, prejudice to the mind, remorse to the conscience, despair to the heart, vicious decisions to the will, and the blindness of passion and fury of destruction to the entire man. Harsh words are the arrows of anger, and the vehicles of death; the weapons of hell, and ebullitions of superficial and unreflective men; they are the scum of malicious and vindictive minds; mark their path, like the lightning, by destruction; goad men to forbidden paths, and are provocative of all kinds of evil; hence, "an angry man stirreth up strife, and a furious man aboundeth in transgression."

Kind words are winged messengers of mercy; the balm of the weary spirit, and incentives to holy deeds; they pass through the waste places of man's soul, like living waters, ever carrying with them both fruitfulness and joy. They are the servants of divine love, who go out into the highways and byways of life to fetch home poor wanderers to partake of the feast of fat things which mercy has provided. Kind words are full of strength to the weak in the battle of life, and of hope to the hopeless on the borders of despair. It is by kind words that the Great Teacher carries light to the dark, joy to the sad, healing to the wounded, courage to the timid, decision to the wavering, and puts weapons into the hands of His disciples, by which they are enabled to conquer both themselves and the world. Kind words have done more to elevate men than science or art, and to preserve them from sin than prisons or gibbets. Kind words are the storehouses of thought, the honey-comb of wisdom, the offspring of self-knowledge, the companion of the chastened and subdued; the wealth, power, and beauty of the poor in spirit; the language of heaven's own children, who, having received mercy, have learnt to be merciful.

Kind words, in the hand of God's Spirit, form, indeed, the bread-seed of heaven's harvest; and, while they impart grace to the lips that utter them, should especially date their birth and parentage from those of the Christian. Let all, therefore, who profess to be such, and especially those who frequently find it difficult to give utterance to words of love, reflect upon what they once were, and would have continued to be, but for the kindness of their great Friend. Let them think of their past conduct, their numberless sins, and forgetfulness of God; the base ingratitude, pride, prejudice, ignorance, and perverseness their Saviour has frequently witnessed in them; how often even now they forsake their own mercy, turn aside from the paths of wisdom, and grieve the Saviour whom they profess to love. Above all, let the disciple of Christ ever remember the unmerited kindness of his Lord; how He met him in love, and taught him in mercy; how He bore with his ignorance, and bound up his wounds; how, through words of kindness, he removed his prejudice, softened his heart, enlightened his conscience, loosened his bonds, and conducted his mind to peace and rest. Thus musing upon the love of Him whose lips drop as the honeycomb, whose words are as a springing well and a flowing brook, the sincere Christian will seek for grace to imitate his Lord, and pray that the law of kindness may so rule his lips that he may be a child

12*

of mercy in the midst of a merciless but sinful
and erring world.

Speak kindly to the broken heart,
   Wrath ne'er the will can bend;
And gentle words have ever proved
   To virtue's cause a friend.

The heavy rain that loudly falls,
   Makes Nature droop her head;
The gentle dew bids her look up,
   And smile as from the dead.

A skilful hand he needs must have,
   Who plays a broken harp;
And Jesus' love must rule the words
   Which heal the stricken heart.

Because our griefs so righteous come,
   And pain the heart must feel,
Should Christians' lips our wounds inflame,
   And say they ne'er shall heal?

Some things our want of skill make hard,
   And all our patience prove;
But hard to Christians should it be,
   To speak the truth in love?

Helpless, though strong, is man at best,
   Oft wrecked on misery's shore;
One unkind word his hope may quench,
   And he is seen no more.

Oh, who that knows himself, and mourns
   His feet oft turned aside;
Who would not pray, if he must speak,
   In gentlest terms to chide?

Oh, who that knows a Saviour's love,
　And joy of sin forgiven;
Who would not seek by words of love,
　To guide a soul to heaven?

Speak kindly to the ear of man,
　He will not turn away;
And thou, some wanderer yet mayst lead
　To realms of endless day!

" There are who mourn for dear ones reft and riven
From out the inmost shrine of loving hearts;
Now shining far perchance like stars of heaven,
But yet the tie, though parted, ever parts;
There are who sorrows weep more drear than this:
Oh, hush, that depth unknown, unsounded is."

REV. E. H. BICKERSTETH.

" Lay thy hand upon thy mouth, brother,
Lay thy hand upon thy mouth;
One word thou hast spoken; but another
Were perhaps too much for truth.
Home is left—oh! yes, if leaving
Be when home is in the heart:
Grieving—yes, 'tis grief, if grieving
Be for those who cannot part.
We are one, brother, we are one.
Since first the golden cloud was spun:
It may lengthen, but it cannot sever,
For, brother, it is twined—and twined for ever."

Ibid.

The Weeping Disciples;

OR,

CONSOLATION FOR THE PARTED.

" And they all wept sore, fell on Paul's neck, and kissed him."—Acts xx. 37.

IT appears needful that the heart of man should be well furrowed by sorrow, in order that the precious seeds of truth may take deep root within, and bear fruit to the praise of his great Creator. It is a cheering thought, however, that the April days of our grief, when sanctified, do but prepare us for a spring-time of joy, and a ripe autumn of spiritual fruitfulness and beauty. Arising out of the nature of things, therefore, it is impossible for those who despise the rod of affliction ever to be wise, or for those who simply weep *without God*, to be possessed of that holy and sublime hope which is the especial heritage of those who are chastened and subdued by Divine mercy.

Among the many things which sadden the heart and fill the eyes with tears, is that of separation from those made dear to us by the ties of natural and spiritual love. The inspired evangelist, in describing the departure of the Apostle Paul from the brethren at Miletus, presents us with an interesting and deeply affecting illustration of this. It is not our intention, however, to dwell upon this incident in the life of this great man, but just briefly to state some few things which may tend to console the Christian under such circumstances. Let him, then, consider that those from whom he is parted *belong to God*, that they are His especial property, and that, redeemed by the blood of His Son and sanctified by His Spirit, He has a greater interest in their well-being and all that concerns them, than any one else, however near and dear to them; and has a right, therefore, to fix the bounds of their habitation, and to determine whether they shall dwell upon the land or the sea, in the solitary and uncultivated wilderness, or the crowded city. Whatever, therefore, our feelings may be, it is our duty to bow to the will of God, and cheerfully to acknowledge that He has a right to do with His own as it may please Him.

It behoves us, therefore, to remember, that whatever we may be called upon to suffer from the absence of those whom we love, it is the mercy and privilege of each child of faith, to have his path, place, and portion below assigned him by his Father's hand. It must be wrong, therefore, to sorrow over those from whom we are parted in the faith, as though the hand of an enemy had torn us asunder, or invincible necessity or blind chance had effected our separation. When called upon, therefore, to part from those dear to us in the Lord, let us not view their lawful avocations, simply as calling them from us, but let us recognise the hand of their God and Father upon them, just selecting them, and guiding them to the place and the work he means them to accomplish. Beholding thus the love which severs, it will mitigate our sorrow, and we shall not dare to oppose its decision. Nor should we forget that the absence of an endeared friend may be sanctified to the bringing our hearts nearer to One who is present at all times, and who by every trial He appoints us, perpetually exclaims, "My son, give me thy heart."

The believer, too, should consider that as his Christian relatives and friends belong to God, they have an especial interest in His love and care; that He has promised to be a wall of fire round about them, and the glory in their midst; that Jesus Himself will be a sanctuary to all who love Him, and that it is declared that nothing shall harm those who are "followers of that which is good." Upon the words of a covenant-keeping God the Christian may therefore rely in peace, when called upon to surrender those whom he loves to a perilous path or a strange country.

The Christian should also bear in mind, that his friends are witnesses for God, lights enkindled by His love to dispel the darkness of men; that wherever they go their example may elevate their fellows, and the seed of truth which they scatter yield a rich fruitage to the glory of their Lord. To accomplish these designs of Divine mercy, many must constantly sail upon the mighty deep and others wander in distant lands. Christian hearts may weep over the inexorable influence of the bread which perisheth, while yet the purposes of God's love are accomplished by His all but homeless children, who are compelled, as it is sometimes said, to travel hither and thither, in obedience to the call of a secular avocation. But oh, Christian! reflect that the one over whose wanderings thou dost mourn so frequently, whose absence thou dost deplore, is an apostle of God's love, and it may be the will of thy Father that he should be frequently taken from thee, to exhibit the truth in the midst of thick darkness, and to bring many wanderers to the feet of his Lord. Should not this mitigate thy sorrow, and constrain thee to pray that each step taken from thee, by those thou dost love, may be but a step towards some poor benighted heart, destined to be the temple of truth and the throne of Jesus.

There is the mercy-seat too, Christian, to which thou canst perpetually go and commune with thine absent one. Neither wind nor wave, storm nor tempest, nearness nor distance, can affect *this:* here thou wilt ever find One who can help and sympathise with thee, and whose love, stronger than death, still binds thy heart to thy absent friend, with a cord no change can break, and whose spirit enkindles in thy heart the immortal hope, that when death shall remove thy frail tabernacle, thou wilt meet with the endeared object of thy Christian love in that holy world where sorrow and parting are unknown.

" Now we must leave our fatherland,
    And wander far o'er ocean's foam ;
Broken is kinship's dearest band,
    Forsaken stands our ancient home ;
But One will ever with us go
    Through busiest day and stillest night ;
The heavens above, the deeps below,
    Shrink back abashed before His sight.

Then be the issue life or death ;
    Let Him do as it seems Him best.
The messenger of Christian faith
    Looks not in this world for his rest.
If but His hand still hold us fast,
    His presence hourly fold us round,
The anchor of our souls is cast
    Firm in the one eternal ground.

The voice of everlasting love
    That rang with living power through us,

13

Is worthy thus our souls to move,
　Worthy to fill a lifetime thus;
Here none was e'er deceived or lost,
　Howe'er his earthly hopes might fade;
Then well for him who weighs the cost
　Ere yet his final choice is made.

Yes, scattered are our brothers now
　O'er land and ocean far apart,
Yet to one Master still they bow,
　In Him they still are one in heart;
For as *one* sin, *one* poison ran
　Through all our race since Adam's fall;
There is *one* hope, *one* life for man
　In Him who bore the sins of all.

Sweet for each other oft to plead,
　And feel our oneness in the Son;
And then we daily meet indeed
　In spirit at our Father's throne!
Our bodies are but parted here,
　And fade in this dark land away.
The earthly shadows disappear,
　The harvest ripens for that day.

Soon Time for us shall cease to reign,
　The Saviour calls us home in peace;
At last we all shall meet again,
　And dwell together all in bliss,
Where faith to clearest vision yields,—
　Triumphant light for sorrowing gloom,
For desert wastes fair Eden's fields,
　For tearful paths a blessed home!"

ALBERT KNAPP,
Lyra Germanica.

"Exhaustless Treasure! Being limitless!
What gaze has ever pierced Thy deep abyss?
Deep Fount of life! Light inaccessible!
How great Thy power, O God, what tongue can tell?

Thy Christendom is singing night and day,
'Glory to Him, the mighty God, for aye,
By Whom, through Whom, in Whom, all beings are!'
Grant us to echo on this song afar."

J. FRANK.

"But how the fallen creature man needs the interior light of
God to strengthen his soul, and the promises of God to sustain
his hope, in every step of his pilgrimage."

M. A. SCHIMMELPENNINCK.

"Who has not seen the sun on a fine spring morning pouring
his rays through a transparent white cloud, filling all places with
the purity of his presence, and kindling the woods into joy and
song. Such, I conceive, would be the constant effects of the
Holy Spirit on the soul, were there no evil in the world. As it
is, the moral sun, like the natural, though it always makes a day,
is often clouded over."—*Guesses at Truth.*

If all our definitions were drawn through our hearts and
steeped in the blood of our own spiritual life, we should be saved
from many mistakes; the hearts of the people would be more
deeply affected, and God's Spirit more abundantly honoured.

The Love of the Spirit;

THE CHURCHES' GREAT NEED.

" The love of the Spirit."—Rom. xv. 30.

THE vast temple of the universe is but the whispering gallery of God's Spirit, but the framework to the costly embroidery of His love. There is no spot below where His voice cannot be heard: no place where the finished creations of His presence and love cannot be seen. Men, however, for the most part, admire the work, but will not see the hand by which it is accomplished; and hear the voice, but pay no regard to the LOVE of which it is the echo. We purpose noticing some few things through which the love of God's Spirit displays itself.

THE COVENANT.—This word has become almost obsolete in modern theology. To our fathers it meant a good deal, to us it means little or nothing.

13*

"This cup is the New Testament in my blood," said the Saviour. "The New Testament, sealed and ratified by the precious blood of Christ, is but a verbal amplification of the covenant of grace. But this book mentioned by our Saviour, with all its provisions and determinations, its doctrines and precepts, must have been in the heart of God before it was drawn out before us through the medium of so many characters and words. The covenant of grace must have been in the infinite mind of the Trinity in Unity before it was told out to us through our finite language; and hence this covenant must be very ancient—yea, co-existent with the very being of God Himself;—and long before the love of God's Spirit imprinted itself upon this visible universe, it was displayed in connection with that covenant which had for its object the salvation of the countless host of God's elect. In answer to the requirements or determinations of that covenant, God's Spirit agreed to become the Quickener and sanctifier of all those embraced by it; to bring them to a knowledge of the Saviour; in a word, to bring together and place upon the one foundation Christ Jesus, all the living stones of that wondrous temple of mercy of which Christ is to be the light and beauty for ever and ever." "For I have said, mercy shall be built up for ever; thy faithfulness shalt thou establish in the very heavens." When we reflect upon the *character* of those who compose this edifice of mercy, how wonderful the love of God's Spirit, that He should deign to *teach* and work with such materials.

CREATION.—" By the breath or Spirit of the Lord, the heavens were made, and all the host of them by the breath of His mouth." He made the sun and the moon, and spangled the heavens with stars; and though the constellations which shine so brightly above us may appear confused, it is only in appearance. Order reigns supreme; and every point of light which meets the eye streaming forth from the vast abysses of space, is but a shining letter in the name of Jehovah written by the omnipotent finger of God's Spirit. The visible heavens may be viewed as the vesture of the Almighty, woven in the loom of infinite wisdom and love by Him who is emphatically the COMFORTER of the church. " He healeth the broken in heart, and bindeth up their griefs. He telleth the number of the stars; he calleth them all by their names. Great is our Lord, and of great power: his understanding is infinite."

This world exhibits the love of God's Spirit also. He it was who originally with outstretched wings, dove-like, brooded over the chaotic elements of this forming world to impregnate them with every form of life, beauty, and beneficence; and so exquisite was His work, that His all-embracing love can be traced in the beating heart of the animalcule as well as the giant limbs of the

elephant. Nor is the love of God's Spirit less
apparent in man: we behold it in the frail but
exquisitely formed temple of his humanity, and
in the immortal inmate within; the earthly but
curiously wrought and elaborated cabinet, with its
hidden jewel, speak eloquently of His love, while
the mind, with all its god-like powers, in various
forms, perpetually and universally repeats the same
tale. The love of God's Spirit, then, streams down
upon us from the heavens above us; is reflected
from every part of the vast temple of the universe
around us; and is pre-eminently exhibited by man
—its great High Priest—the marvellous balance
and ceaseless activity of whose powers were intended perpetually to hymn forth its praise. As,
therefore, all things below exhibit the love of
God's Spirit, all are called upon to praise Him.
"Praise the Lord," says the Psalmist, "from the
earth, ye dragons, and all deeps; fire, and hail;
snow, and vapours; stormy wind fulfilling His
word; mountains, and all hills; fruitful trees, and
all cedars; beasts, and all cattle; creeping things,
and flying fowl; kings of the earth, and all people;
princes, and all judges of the earth. Both young
men and maidens; old men and children: let
them praise the name of the Lord: for His name
alone is excellent; His glory is above the earth
and heaven."

PROVIDENCE.—As God's Spirit is above the
world of matter, so He is also above the world of

mind; and His love is seen sustaining and directing the former, and in ruling and restraining the
latter. God's Spirit is more than equal to all the
designs of men. Could but one thought get from
beneath his fingers, or slip from the tongue, or get
into a book without His knowledge or the control
of His love, what a hell of misery the world
would speedily become! But earth and hell perpetually recognise His supremacy and control.

REDEMPTION.—1. *Incarnation of Christ.*—To
the Spirit of God was entrusted the formation of
the sacred temple of our Saviour's humanity. Oh,
what a temple was this! And not only so, but
that immortal spirit, which was a lucid mirror of
the moral perfections of God from the cradle to
the tomb, with all its costly furniture, its moral
beauty and mental opulence. Talk they of the music of the soul, what a hymn of delight, a strain of
pure, harmonious, ravishing music must the Spirit
of Jesus perpetually have sent forth to God! the
centre of moral force and power; the conscience
never darkened or crippled by sin; the will and
affections never at variance; so perfect and infallible a balance of all the powers maintained, that
however dark, confused, and disturbed the outward life might be yea, dark as that which fell
upon the land of Egypt when God smote their
first-born, there was ever the light of purity,
peace, and full conformity to God's law within—
a light which all the waves of tribulation could

not dim, much less put out; but which burnt brightest beneath the hidings of His Father's face, and the floods of indescribable anguish and death which closed His earthly career. That the Spirit of God should thus, for our sakes, have formed the man Christ Jesus, and so wondrously and mysteriously have veiled the glories of His divinity beneath the vesture of our perfected humanity, that so, though fallen, we might have some faint idea of what truly belongs to us as made by God, and of what that God is to whom we are indebted for our existence, and by whose grace alone we can be restored again to His image and love, abundantly declares the love of God's Spirit. In the person Christ, then, we see that the Spirit of God could make an intellect which should never err—a will whose volitions should ever command the approbation of God—a conscience without self-rebuke—a heart that should never embrace sin—a memory which should never present a stain of personal defilement—for all these were found in Him who was despised of men— the most perfect human sympathies with the very perfections of God. How great the love of God's Spirit thus to work for our redemption!

2. *The Anointing of Christ.*—Our Saviour was anointed of the Spirit, to preach the Gospel to the meek.—Isa. lxi. 1. And from the same Almighty source " The tongue of the learned was given to Him, that he might know how to speak a word in

season to the weary;" and as the High Priest under the law was known by his unction, which was not to be imitated, so Jesus is known to the contrite and broken in spirit by the unctious words of divine peace and consolation which He only can speak to the heart. Oh, what love of the Spirit, thus to anoint Him to minister to our woes!

Of our Saviour, too, it was declared that " He was anointed with the oil of gladness above His fellows;" and this oil of gladness or joy of the Lord was His strength. It was the Spirit of God who comforted and supported Him beneath all His sorrows, and led Him forth to all His terrible conflicts with the powers of darkness, and hence we read, "Then was Jesus led of the Spirit into the 'wilderness to be tempted of the devil;"—and the same loving and Almighty friend who led Him forth to this great conflict with the powers of darkness, was with Him to sustain and crown Him with final victory. Yes, even the man Christ Jesus was clothed in celestial panoply by God's Spirit, who put the sword of truth into His hand, and so anointed the shield of His faith, that all the fiery darts of Satan glanced off and fell at His feet.

3. *The Sufferings and Death of Christ.*—All through the strange and varied sorrows of His life Christ had a secret and abiding source of strength and joy in the anointing of God's Spirit; *this* He

could not lose; alas, for us, had it been possible. The covenant of grace ensured it to Him in His complex character, and hence, though deserted by His disciples in the midst of His great and sore travail, He was never utterly forsaken. The Spirit of God, His companion through life, was still with Him to cheer and sustain. And when the dread moment came that His sacred humanity upheld by his Godhead must bear and exhaust all the bitter elements of that curse which our sins had entailed, in the midst of all the darkness, and wounds, and agony, and blood, and exhaustion, and woe, and weariness, and sighs, and cries, and tears, and fainting, and death, God's Spirit was there to whisper words of consolation, and to enable Him to say in peace at last, "It is finished!"

4. *The Resurrection of Christ.*—"Thou wilt not leave my soul in Ades, neither wilt Thou suffer Thine Holy One to see corruption." The same Almighty Spirit who anointed Christ, and watched over Him with an unslumbering eye all through the various scenes of His life, with sleepless vigilance watched over the sacred temple of His humanity when hanging on the Cross, and when placed in the tomb. Oh, with what love did He look upon that frail but exquisitely wrought vessel of shell through which the hidden treasure of God's love, mercy, wisdom, and power had been put forth for the salvation of myriads; and with

what joy when the predicted moment came would He raise it from the tomb! What a sight through the love of God's Spirit would burst upon the vision of the glorified, when Jesus, through the Eternal Spirit, took possession of His throne, robed in the garments of light and immortality, to fill heaven with His redeemed, and their hearts with bliss and blessedness for ever and ever!

> "O mighty Spirit! source whence all things spring!.
> O glorious Majesty of perfect light!
> Hath ever worthy praise to Thee been sung,
> Or mortal heart endured to meet thy sight?
> If they who sin have never known
> Must veil their faces at Thy throne,
> Oh, how shall I, who am but sin and dust,
> Approach untrembling to the Pure and Just?"

We have hitherto dwelt upon the love of the Spirit as displayed *without* the church, and how feeble have been our attempts to set forth some of its wonderful and manifold expressions; it remains for us now to notice His love as it shines resplendent within the church, and is made known IN THE EXPERIENCE OF THE BELIEVER.—To the love of God's Spirit the believer owes that he is called to a knowledge of Christ, of himself,.and the truth. By nature he is a child of wrath, even as others, ignorant of God and at enmity with Him, and in this state he would live and die were it not that in due time the Spirit in love clothes

14

the word with divine power, throws light into the
dark mind, slays the enmity and pride which reign
within, and brings the convicted mind with weeping and supplication to the footstool of mercy.
Hence, says the Apostle, " Knowing, brethren beloved, your election of God, for our gospel came
not unto you in word only, but in power and in
the Holy Ghost, and in much assurance." The
voice of God's Spirit, therefore, is a mighty voice,
but full of love, for it is intended to sever from
sin, and to guide the arrested spirit to heaven.
The call of God's Spirit, therefore, is spoken of
as "high and holy;" it confers great dignity and
elevation of character, leads to the most high
God, and to love of holiness.

And the voice of God's Spirit which calls,
brings *life:* "I give unto my sheep eternal life,"
said Christ, but He gives this life by His Spirit;
"and you hath he quickened," says the Apostle,
"who were dead in trespasses and sins;" this life
shows itself in conviction of sin, under the influence of which the mind turns to the light which
manifests its darkness and condemns it, and spiritual sensibility, under the influence of which
godly sorrow for sin is produced. Thus, by the
love of God's Spirit, the ancient promise becomes
a verity in the experience; "I will take away
the heart of stone, and give a heart of flesh."

The manner also in which the Spirit does this
work displays His love; kindly and gently and

progressively does he remove our darkness, and discover to our astonished gaze the secrets of the charnel-house within; enabling us by degrees to decipher the manifold characters of *death* inscribed by sin upon the chambers of imagery, and contemporaneously imparting a knowledge of Him who came to seek and to save, so that the mind is kept from despair. Those, therefore, who have been wounded by God's Spirit know that He wounds but to heal, and reveals our moral malady but to lead to the Great Physician.

To the same Almighty source and wondrous love we owe our pardon; for although this is procured by "Jesus, in whom we have redemption through His blood, the forgiveness of sins according to the riches of His grace," it is the Spirit who brings this precious jewel from the heart of Jesus, and makes it ours by giving us faith to believe. To the same love also we owe our justification and adoption, for the hand which by faith sprinkles the blood upon the conscience brings us that righteousness on the ground of which we are accounted just before God;· a righteousness so pure "that an angel's tear would stain it, and the blood of the holiest martyrs would defile it;" so perfect that even God himself, beholding His people in it, declares them to be faultless, without spot or wrinkle, or any such thing; a righteousness more glorious than that of the highest archangel—for his is but a creature righteousness,

while this is indeed the RIGHTEOUSNESS OF
GOD!

But not only does God's Spirit reveal these
precious things to us, but Christ Himself, in
whom are hid all the treasures of wisdom and
knowledge.   Hence the Apostle prayed for his
brethren that "the spirit of wisdom and revelation" might be given to them, "in the knowledge
of Him."   This is the highest of all knowledge we
can seeek or have from the love of God's Spirit.
Christ is the mirror of the Godhead, and embodies
all created and uncreated glory in Himself; and
when the Spirit enlightens the mind, He ever
throws the rays of truth upon the face of Him
who is the fairest of the fair, the brightness of the
divine glory, and the express image of His person.
It is not sufficient that Christ is in the word; He
must be revealed to and enthroned in the hearts
of those whom He saves, and until He is seen in
the light of the Spirit He will never be embraced,
and unless thus embraced there can never be
peace.   For every glimpse of Christ's glory, for
every taste of His love, for every perception of
His varied excellences, we are indebted to the
love of God's Spirit.   Oh, think of what He is,
believer; of the precious truths and promises
which centre in Him, of His personal glories, His
unsearchable riches, and acquired dominion; and
then remember that thou wouldst never have
known Him or called Him thine but for the love

of God's Spirit. Oh, think that but for the love
of God's Spirit, this sun might have shone while
yet your spirit had never rejoiced in its light;
this rose might have bloomed while yet its fragrance had never reached you; this fountain
might have flowed, while yet its living. waters
slaked not your thirst: with what adoration and
love, therefore, ought we to yield ourselves to the
influence of God's Spirit!

Our *sanctification*, too, we owe to God's Spirit;
He who brings pardon and righteousness *from*
Jesus conforms us *to* Jesus; and oh, what love
shines in this work! He *does* "purge away our
dross and take away our sin," but how kindly
does He accomplish it. We should wonder at and
admire the lapidary who could handle with such
exquisite tenderness and skill those minute but
beautiful shells which the microscope reveals so
as to bring out their latent colours and beauties;
how much more should we admire the work of
the Great Sanctifier, who, although He fastened
the pillars of the universe, preserves unbroken in
His hands the frail vessels of mercy, yea, even
polishes and beautifies them. Strange that He
should write the great name of Christ upon such
little things. We marvel at the light which, flying
through the regions of space, brings the pictures of
such vast bodies to paint them upon the eye; how
much more marvellous is that light which God's
Spirit in love transmits to the soul to restore the

14*

image of heaven's King and Lord of all worlds.
But, oh, the wisdom, patience, and long-suffering
of God's Spirit, developed in bringing out the
image of Christ upon the soul! What ignorance,
stupidity, impatience, and rebellion He has to contend with in the prosecution of His loving work!
With what exquisite yet invincible tenderness
does He *wrench* the mind from its idols, scatter its
prejudices, and bring it by degrees to embrace the
humbling doctrines of the Cross! How constantly does He watch over the graces which He
implants, preserving them lively and active amid
the moral contagion of the world, the nipping
frosts of affliction, the cold blasts of persecution,
poverty, bereavement, and pain; enabling the
believer to glory even in tribulation, "knowing
that tribulation worketh patience, and patience
experience, and experience hope." O Blessed
Spirit, in Thy great LOVE sanctify us wholly!
amid the atmosphere of Atheism which surrounds
us help us to breathe after God; and when encompassed by corruption, oh grant us strength to
maintain our purity! While passing through the
vanity fair of this world, enable us to walk as
kings and priests unto God, to exhibit the fair
mitre of holiness, and to manifest a faithful and
right loyal spirit to our Lord. When Satan, too,
assaults us, clothe Thou us in celestial panoply,
and by the weapons Thou hast provided for us
help us to put him to flight. O teach us how to

war a good warfare, to fight the fight of faith, to perfect holiness, to lay hold on eternal life!

Perseverance.—It is to the love of God's Spirit we owe that all the epistles of His mercy are not destroyed, or the truths which they are intended to exhibit so obliterated as to answer no purpose but to puzzle and bewilder poor erring men. It is the love of God's Spirit which lights all the lamps of his temple, and it is the same love which prevents their being extinguished by Satan. It is the love of God's Spirit which starts the Christian on his journey, and preserves him to the end. He it is who strengthens him when weak, comforts him when sad, and restores his soul again and again. O believer, thy faith had long ere this been paralysed, despair had seized thee, Satan had spoiled thee, but for the love of God's Spirit. To Him thou dost owe every good thought, every heart-cheering visitation from God, thy assurance of interest in His love, and joy in thy Lord. Thou wast once an alien, He made thee a child; once a slave, He made thee a son; once a rebel, He transformed thee to a friend. He made thy body His temple, thy heart the throne of Christ, thy memory the storehouse of His love, thy intellect the home of heavenly wisdom, and thy tongue the instrument of His praise; and yet thou hast frequently grieved, slighted, and resisted Him. Oh, how great the love which has borne with thee, reclaimed thee,

renewed thee; and notwithstanding all thy pro-
vocations, forgetfulness, and ingratitude, would
not forsake thee! Oh, if thou canst contemplate
this love without weeping eyes, how hard thy
heart; if this love does not beget love in thee,
how desperate thy condition! O Spirit of Love,
increase our obligations again to Thee, and

" Shed abroad a Saviour's love, and that shall kindle ours."

Glorification.—The gems polished by the hand
of God's Spirit, He will set in the Saviour's crown;
the vessel of mercy moulded and elaborated by
Him, He will place in the palace of heaven's King.
He who in love raised the sacred humanity of
Christ from the tomb to a throne of glory, will
accomplish the same work for all for whom Christ
has died. Seest thou, believer, the Sun of Righteousness in heaven, and the bright mirrors which
perpetually catch and reflect its rays; think then
of the love which brightened and placed them
there! Dost thou behold the innumerable host
redeemed in shining raiment, faultless before the
throne of God, and dost thou hear the mighty
song they raise, like the sound of many waters,
and which perpetually fills the ears of Him, who
thus for ever shall inhabit the praises of eternity;
then while thy heart exalts the Lamb, whose
death procured the life of myriads, and peopled
the vast plains of heaven with the victorious co-

horts of the redeemed from every nation, and
kingdom, and tongue, the realms of desolation,
sin, and sorrow, forget not the love of God's
Spirit, displayed in the life, the triumph, the perfection, and exaltation of them all, and magnify
Him for so glorious, visible, everlasting, and triumphant a consummation of the gracious, godlike
determination, " AND ALL THY CHILDREN SHALL
BE TAUGHT OF JEHOVAH, AND GREAT SHALL BE
THE PEACE OF THY CHILDREN !"—It has been
said, that in all God gives, He forgives ; and may
He forgive us, that while He has given unto us
these perceptions of the love of His Spirit, our
love is so feeble, and our praise so faint. But
seeing we are so indebted to the love of His
Spirit, let us now contemplate the influence it
should exert upon us; and should it not constrain us to *reciprocate His love*, by holy and
constant obedience, by childlike confidence, by
listening to His voice, His gentle admonitions,
and the corrections of His faithful love through
the word; by yielding ourselves to His influence, and glorying in our weakness that His
power may rest upon us ; by taking heed that
we grieve Him not by vain thoughts, evil
tempers, or sinful imaginations ; by prizing every
truth He makes known, every ray of light He
transmits, and, above all, by cleaving to that
Saviour whom He loves to exalt ; by seeking to
discover and by treasuring up in our minds all

the various pledges of His love, each holy thought
and hallowed hour, and by aiming perpetually to
turn them into occasions for adoring gratitude
and praise; by seeking to have His wisdom incarnate in our thoughts and words, and His sweet
refreshing influence like the morning dew perpetually upon our hearts; by aiming to exhibit that
Saviour whom He loves to reveal, and whose words
form the seed of eternal life which he perpetually
waters; by seeking His help and teaching at all
times and under all circumstances, at home and
abroad, especially when engaged in secret or
public prayer, searching the Scriptures, preaching
or listening to the proclamation of the Gospel; by
watching the unfoldings of His love in the spiritual
experience of which He is the Author, and by
treating with holy reverence His work, both in
ourselves and others. Oh that we may be jealous
for His glory, and never ashamed to confess our
dependence upon His teaching and help! How
sad it is to hear men who profess to owe all that
they are spiritually to the love of God's Spirit,
indulging in such a style of phraseology as completely hides His person and the glory of His
work; oh that the love of God's Spirit may so
constrain His servants, that they may cease to hide
God's living Spirit beneath their cold, vague,
abstract, philosophic terms, and study with an
agony of love to find out such words as shall exalt
His divine personality and most glorious work!

Let us bear in mind that He can constantly make the Bible a *new* book, and cause the truth He makes known to us to grow in us, and expand like a living and fruitful tree; while mere intellectual power and resources are soon exhausted and run themselves dry. In the service of the sanctuary, God's Spirit is the only well-spring of spiritual power, freshness, variety, wisdom, beauty, and truth; and as Nature requires the baptism of the clouds, and the morning dews, in order to her life and fruitfulness, so the servant of Christ needs to have his mind bathed again and again in the living waters of God's Spirit, and for the healing, vivifying, and refreshing dew of His love to freshen all his mental powers, and invigorate his faith, or he will soon stand like a barren tree in the garden of God; for unless our gifts are fed by the Spirit of God, they will soon wither like leaves severed from the tree on which they grew. We live in a day of much excitement, and knowledge is greatly on the increase; but let us not deceive ourselves, unless there is a more *practical* faith in the presence and power of God's Spirit, and earnest prayer for His blessing, the wilderness of this world will never be made to rejoice and blossom as the rose.

"Sweetest joy the soul can know
Fairest light was ever shed,
Who alike in joy or woe
Leavest none unvisited;

Spirit of the highest God,
Lord, from whom is life bestow'd,
Who upholdest everything,
Hear me, hear me while I sing!

For the noblest gift Thou art
     That a soul e'er sought or won
Have I wish'd Thee to my heart,
     Then my wishing all is done.
Ah! then yield Thee, nor refuse
Here to dwell, for thou didst choose
This my heart, from e'en its birth,
For Thy temple here on earth.

Thou art shed like gentlest showers
     From the Father and the Son,
Bringest to this earth of ours
     Purest blessing from their throne.
Suffer then, O noble Guest,
That rich gift by Thee possesst,
That Thou givest at Thy will
All my soul and flesh to fill.

Thou art wise, before Thee stand
     Hidden things unveil'd to Thee,
Countest up the grains of sand,
     Fathomest the deepest sea.
And Thou knowest well how blind,
Dark, and crooked is my mind.
Give me wisdom in Thy light,
Let me please my God aright.

Thou art holy; enterest in
     Where pure hearts Thy coming wait;
But Thou flee'st shame and sin,
     Craft and falsehood Thou dost hate.

Wash me then, O Well of Grace,
Every stain and spot efface;
Let me flee what Thou dost flee,
Grant me what Thou lov'st to see.

Thou art loving, hatest strife;
    As a lamb of patient mood,
Calm through all our restless life,
    Even to sinners kind and good.
Grant me, too, this noble mind,
To be calm, and true, and kind,
Loving every friend or foe,
Grieving none whom Thou dost know.

Well contented is my heart,
    If but Thou reject me not;
If but Thou wilt ne'er depart,
    I am blest whate'er my lot.
Thine for ever make me now,
And to Thee, my Lord, I vow,
Here and yonder to employ
Every power for Thee with joy.

Be my help when danger's nigh;
    When I sink hold Thou me up;
Be my life when I must die,
    In the grave be Thou my hope.
Bring me when I rise again
To the land that knows no pain,
Where Thy followers from Thy stream
Drink for ever joys supreme."

PAUL GERHARDT. 1635.
Lyra Germanica.

15

" Still nigh me, O my Saviour, stand,
    And guard in fierce temptation's hour,
Hide in the hollow of Thy hand,
    Show forth in me Thy saving power ;
Still be Thine arm my sure defence,
Nor earth nor hell shall pluck me thence.

In suffering, be Thy love my peace ;
    In weakness, be Thy love my power.
And when the storms of life shall cease,
    Jesus, in that important hour,
In death, as life, be Thou my guide,
And save me, who for me hath died."

" Satan, in his temptations, strikes principally at the *faith* of
God's people, that being the grace which gives most glory to God,
and in the exercise of which believers have much peace, joy, and
comfort; and it is also a shield which keeps off and quenches his
fiery darts, and therefore he endeavours all he can to weaken and
destroy it, or wrest it out of their hands."   DR. GILL.

The Disciple Admonished;

OR,

THE CHRISTIAN'S DANGER.

" And the Lord said, Simon, Simon, behold Satan hath desired to have you, that he may sift you as wheat : but I have prayed for thee, that thy faith fail not: and when thou art converted, strengthen thy brethren."—Luke xxii. 31, 32.

THESE words must have fallen with terrible emphasis upon the ears of Peter. In the present pseudo-philosophical age, the doctrine of Satanic influence is either altogether ignored or referred to as a myth belonging to the dark ages of the world's history. With what awful solemnity, however, does our Saviour refer to it, and how the heart of Peter must have quailed before His words; to be told by the lips that never err that the great adversary had an especial desire for his destruction, how fearful, how awful! Why, it was like telling him that he stood upon the mouth of hell, and that the flames of the bottomless pit were spreading around him ; and had not the Lord

added the consolatory words, " but I have prayed
for thee," the dreadful intelligence would doubtless have pressed him down to despair.   And
what, reader, would be your feelings were such
language addressed to you ?   Would it not make
you tremble to be told by the God who made you,
that the Lion of hell was watching you, especially
with a view to your present and everlasting
destruction ?   Be it known to you, then, that thus
you are addressed ; for does not His book inform
us that the " great Evil One" " goeth about as a
roaring lion, seeking whom he may devour?"
And who can tell how soon he may cross your
path, and you may be crushed in his awful embrace?   No doubt Satan's thoughts have embraced you in common with others, though as yet
you have not felt the sting of his perfected
designs.   Let us, therefore, prayerfully contemplate some few of the truths presented to our view
by this solemn admonition from the lips of the
Great Teacher.

The Omniscience of Christ.—It is interesting to
contemplate Christ gazing upon the material
world as it spread around him, and exhorting His
disciples to consider the lilies of the field, and to
listen to the good news they proclaimed; to hear
His voice giving utterance to the language of
flowers, and to behold Him spreading them before
His disciples as the mute expositors of His Father's love: but He appears more sublime and

impressive as we behold Him looking into the
invisible world and marking the movements of
man's terrible adversary—gazing upon that fallen
spirit whose footsteps though so noiseless, are ever
attended by so much mischief and desolation to
men. Yes, not only did the panorama of this
world paint itself upon the eye of Christ, but the
persons and doings of an unseen world were
reflected there. He looked upon Satan, He held
his chain, and marked his every step; the heaving
of his heart, the beating of his pulse, as by an
electric chord, was communicated to His hand,
and He knew how and when to loosen or to
tighten his bonds; for while the hand was frail
the power was divine. Christ looked upon Satan,
did we say? more, He looked *within* him; the
very heart of the Devil was open to his eye—all
the dark chambers of that infernal palace were
open to Him, He walked through them at His
pleasure—all the wards of that intricate and mysterious lock were perceived by Him, and He could
fit a key to them at His pleasure; deep as was the
fountain of evil within that dark heart, He could
fathom its secret depths; desperately wicked as
was that heart, He knew its every device, could
unravel all those subtle and ingenious threads,
intended to entangle the feet of His saints; He
watched their painful and elaborate production in
that prolific house of misery and sin, and, as often
as it pleased Him, put His fingers upon the cocoons

15*

of hell before the objects to be accomplished by
them were effected. The nets intended for the
birds of paradise He frequently destroyed, and
many half-formed purposes of ill to His church
He crushed in their birth. Beneath piles of Satanic produce, hidden in the most secret recesses of
Satan's bosom, He saw coiled up the viper of
burning hatred, whose especial vocation was to be
the ruin of His servant Peter, and He put His
foot upon its head at once. "I have prayed for
thee." Here was the dart that touched its life,
and placed it beneath the feet of the impulsive
but loving disciple. Oh, to be surrounded by
such a wall of fire, to be shielded by the breath of
Omnipotence, and made invulnerable by the cries
and tears of the Son of God! And let us not
forget that what Jesus did for His servant in days
that are passed, He does for His disciples in every
age ; all are embraced in His petitions, and preserved by His prayers ; like. as the earth is surrounded by the air which ministers to the life of
every living thing, so the intercession of Jesus
perpetually embraces His church, and brings to
her all those elements of truth, succour, and consolation which are essential to her spiritual life
and preservation.

THE DANGER PERCEIVED."—*Satan has desired
to have thee.*"—The desires of Satan are vast and
destructive ; he desires to have all men, but especially the saints. These are the flowers of God's

garden, and he loves to pull them up; the lamps of God's temple, and he would fain blow them out; the epistles of divine truth, and he is ever anxious to tear them to pieces; the golden vessels of the upper sanctuary, destined for ever to reflect God's praise and his disgrace, and hence he seeks perpetually to mar their beauty. Mere professors cost Satan but little trouble and seldom excite his ire; they mostly sleep in his arms, and he carries them where he pleases without trouble; their words, for the most part, accord with his will, and their lamp has no light to expose his designs; but all true Christians he hates, because they belong to Christ, love Christ, exhibit Christ, and fight for Christ; because they expose his designs, pierce him with the truth, and frequently conquer him by their prayers. Now the danger of Christians, as arising from their great adversary, is to be traced chiefly to two things; the character of their foe, and the failure of their faith.

The character of their foe.—Satan is not omniscient, but he has great knowledge; our acquaintance with ourselves may be very superficial, but it is not so with Satan. There may be but very little introspection with him, for what can he see within himself but misery? But he has a peculiar desire to look into man—has made him his especial study, and age after age has accumulated all kinds of information respecting him; and as the result, most men are better known to their great adversary than to themselves. This might well fill them with terror, and would, if they fully believed it. Most men, however, laugh at Satan's chains while they wear them. Philosophic pride may think itself quite able to fortify the soul against all danger, while Satan laughs at its efforts, and sits smiling in the midst of its fruitless labours. Living age after age, man's great foe seldom witnesses anything new, whilst his vast memory, with the experience of the past, can supply him in a moment with a suitable weapon, wherewith to bring down any foe. The heart of man may be deep, but he can find his way into its most secret recesses, and is perfectly at home amid all its unfoldings: hence, while man is often an enigma to himself, his arch enemy reads him with the greatest ease, and will ever present the right bait at the right time; and while his knowledge is ever accurate, practical, profound, and present, it does not terrify him. He has but to look within for the darkest and most bloody episodes of this world's history; but the sight of it does not unnerve him or divert him from his purpose. He has been accumulating wrath against the day of wrath, age after age, but still he works on, nor does the awful mound paralyse him. He delights in cruelty; and hence with the arrows of the Almighty in him, he loves to inflict pain. He has witnessed the tears, the cries, and despairing and dying agonies of myriads, not only without pain, but with joy. He is persevering, too, in the accomplishment of his designs; whoever may sleep, he never does, but by night and day, at all times, and under all circumstances, he works on for the destruction of men. Arising out of his knowledge, cruelty, and perseverance, he has great power; so that even those who have been helped to conquer him, have mostly had to feel and to acknowledge the weight of his hand. This fact our Saviour brings before us, in the figure he employs. "Satan has desired to have thee, that he may sift thee as wheat." Just as easily as a strong man tosses about wheat in a sieve, so easily does Satan toss men about under the influence of temptation. What a forcible illustration we have of this in the life of Peter; had not the intercession of his Lord grasped the hand of his great adversary, with what ease would he have tossed him into hell, as he has done numbers even while in the very act of denying his power. While thus contemplating man's weakness in contrast with Satanic power, with what a solemn emphasis do the words of Christ fall upon the ear, " Simon, Simon, behold Satan hath desired to have thee, that he may sift thee as wheat."

" Ah, Simon, thou art full of love, and zeal, and self-confidence, but alas! alas! shouldst thou be left for a single moment, did my prayers cease to embrace thee, thy weakness would soon appear, and thy soul would be lost. The enemy would

put his hand upon thee, and thy ruin would be
sealed." Dear reader, does not thy soul shrink
within thee lest thou shouldst be so left? Oh,
think of the numbers who have fallen in a moment,
and that to rise no more. Oh, think of their tears
and confessions; they meditated not the deed
which destroyed them, but Satan was at hand,
and they believed it not, and down they went.
Trifle not with temptation; fly for thy life at
once, O reader, to the strong for strength.

But, after all, our great danger arises from another source, the failure of our faith. "I have prayed
for thee," said Christ, "that thy faith fail not."
While the hand of faith grasps its shield we are
safe, the fiery darts of our great enemy fall harmless at our feet; but this hand, it seems, may, for
a time be paralysed, and so leave us open and
exposed to the assaults of our dreaded foe. Here,
then, we have that which is more to be feared than
Satan himself. Oh, ye who have no faith, what will
ye do in the day of battle? do ye not perceive how
certain it is, that unless this shield is thine the
battle must prevail against thee? "Fight the good
fight of faith," said a good soldier of the Cross; but
if thou hast not faith, how canst thou fight? Here
is thy weakness, reader; for it is faith that saves
us. Dost thou inquire how? By teaching us to
have no confidence in ourselves, but great confidence in God; by taking us to the blood of Christ
for the forgiveness of our sins; and His righteous-

ness for the justification of our persons; by helping
us to realize the presence of God—and who can sin
in His presence?—by fetching in fresh strength,
and enabling us to watch, wait, and pray. But
now mark, dear reader, while faith through these
means bruises Satan beneath thy feet, thou mayest not praise thy faith, deify thy faith, attach
merit to thy faith; thy faith saves thee because
Christ prays and prevails, because He lives. " I
have prayed that thy faith fail not." We cannot be saved without faith, but Christ gives it,
and His intercession is the root of its strength.
Faith works, but works by *love*, and Jesus finds
this and keeps it alive. Like Peter, we sometimes
forget to pray, forget to watch; but oh, what a
mercy Jesus does not! His eye never sleeps, His
arm never grows weary, His lips never falter, but
the sweet incense of His adorable intercession constantly ascends before the throne, and hence His
people live. This explains how it is, believer,
that thou hast been helped to persevere, and in-
forms thee why thy faith has not become a withered blasted thing, and thy life as barren as thy
faith; how, though often cast down, thou hast not
been destroyed, though often wounded thou hast
not been killed. Oh, then, while you watch and
pray, and seek as for your life that your faith fail
not, see to it that the praise of its strength and its
victories be given to Him who is its great Author
and Finisher!

But, dear reader, what if thou hast not faith? Then thou hast no Intercessor? What words can describe thy danger; art thou not afraid, dost thou not tremble at the thought of being left in the hands of him who has ruined myriads? Art thou a match for him who is the prince of the power of the air? art thou equal to his knowledge, power, cruelty, and perseverance? Oh, let him but loosen upon thee the full blast of temptation, and, unaided of God, all thy fancied strength, wisdom, and courage will be torn to pieces, and fly like a spider's web before the whirlwind. Fly thou to Christ, let Him be thy shield and buckler, and teach thee how to conquer him who otherwise must be thy victor and lord.

But if we have learnt these truths for ourselves, there is a duty incumbent upon us. "And when thou art converted, strengthen thy brethren," said Christ; "tell them never to despair, that I can subdue their temptations, and preserve them from the tempter; proclaim my love and faithfulness; let the weak, the timid, and the doubting hear how I saved thee from the hand of the spoiler; I have restored thee, go thou and restore others; I have bound up thy wounds, go thou and bind up the wounds of others. Dost thou see men rushing forth like moths towards the fire of hell, warn them of their danger, and inform them of your escape." Thus Jesus teaches and exhorts His servants, especially those whose backslidings

He heals, and who are restored by His grace.
Our plan is to keep the gold from the fire; His
plan is to bring it through the furnace that it may
the more abundantly reflect His praise.   Our plan
is to fill the mouth with words; His to fill the
mind with thoughts and the heart with love.
" Prayer, temptation, and meditation," still make
the ministers of Christ; let us pray, therefore,
for such, and entreat the Lord to send forth men
who, being thus qualified of Himself, shall be
able to speak to the hearts of both saint and sinner, that so both may be profited and saved.

> " Thou seest my feebleness;
>   Jesus, be Thou my power,
> My help and refuge in distress,
>   My fortress and my tower

> Give me to trust in Thee;
>   Be Thou my sure abode;
> My horn, and rock, and buckler be,
>   My Saviour and my God.

> Myself I cannot love,
>   Myself I cannot keep,
> But strength in Thee I surely have,
>   Whose eyelids never sleep.

> My soul, to Thee alone
>   Now, therefore, I commend;
> Thou, Jesus, love me as Thine own,
>   And love me to the end."

16

"Cling to the Crucified:
His death is life to thee—
Life for eternity!
His pains thy pardon seal;
His stripes thy bruises heal;
His cross proclaims thy peace,
Bids every sorrow cease.
His blood is all to thee,
It purges thee from sin;
It sets thy spirit free,
It keeps thy conscience clean.
Cling to the Crucified!

Cling to the Crucified:
His is a heart of love,
Full as the hearts above;
Its depths of sympathy
Are all awake for thee.
His countenance is light,
Even in the darkest night.
That love shall never change,
That light shall ne'er grow dim.
Charge thou thy faithless heart
To find its all in Him.
Cling to the Crucified!"

"Meditate much and often on the sufferings of your Lord. You may thus need less personal suffering to teach you to hate the sin that caused them. In all His afflictions be thou afflicted. Be not estranged in sympathy from the best friend of your soul. Live only to be like Him. Let the first desire of your heart be fixed on the attainment of holiness."—*Christ on the Cross.*

Footsteps of Love;

OR,

JESUS CRUCIFIED.

The Agony in the Garden.

"And being in an agony he prayed more earnestly : and his sweat was as it were great drops of blood falling down to the ground."—Luke xxii. 44.

How little can we understand of the sufferings of Jesus! Into the sacred sanctuary of His sorrows who dares to enter? Our best attemps to come near to Him leave us standing at a distance, gazing upon Him afar off. The sea of His grief was deep, and we behold Him tossed to and fro as by an unseen hand, but we hear very little of the fury of the storm. A shallow, superficial nature heaves and roars beneath the slightest breeze of affliction; but the holy nature of Jesus, calm and deep at all times, scarcely utters a moan amid the terrors of the most dreadful storm. Very few and slight are the intimations of His sorrows, who was most emphatically "a man of sorrows, and acquainted with grief." From His own lips we can gather but little to guide us over the dark and dreadful sea where for a time He appeared to drift, forsaken, naked, desolate, and alone. The great ocean of His anguish was too deep to utter its voice. Its great waves heave and roll on beneath the eye in awful majesty and silence. Jesus seldom spoke while all the waves and billows of God's wrath were passing over Him, and of the meaning of the few words which He did utter we can apprehend but little. His grief was too deep for tears, too great for words. "Behold," said one of old, "and see if there be any sorrows like unto my sorrow." No doubt the sorrows of this good man were great; still we could have understood them, and felt for him, for he was a man, like unto ourselves. But Jesus —the holy, the pure, the unselfish Jesus—how can we appreciate His? And yet it is right that we should strive to apprehend at least a little of His sorrows, for they were the sorrows of humanity, and most emphatically our own. He bore our griefs and carried our sorrows; "the chastisement of our peace was upon him; and with his stripes we are healed." May the Holy Spirit guide our meditations!

"*And being in an agony he prayed more fervently.*" What could be the cause of His anguish? As yet His back was not given to the scourge, nor His sacred temples to the thorns. His quivering flesh shrunk not as yet from the rugged nails; nor was His body oppressed by His weighty cross. What could it be, then? Ah, there was a Hand present, administering the elements of a bitter cup, which no human eye could perceive. There was a pressure from the hand of God which no soul could feel but His own. "It pleased the Father to bruise him." Jesus suffered not simply as a man, but as the Surety of His people. Their sins were upon Him by imputation, and the hand of His Father's justice must inflict the penalty. Already some few drops of the coming storm have fallen upon His holy soul, and amazed, and prostrate, and full of agony unutterable, He falls to the ground. His very pores weep blood. O sin, sin, sin! what hast thou done? This is thy dreadful work;—'twas thou, my soul—thy sins which brought the Father's hand upon His Son, until He weeps and cries, "If it be possible, let this cup pass away." He saw in the distance the cruel soldiery, the purple robe, the crown of thorns, the weary journey, the infuriated crowd, the lingering, protracted death; but it was not the apprehension of these which filled His soul with agony,—there were deeper wounds than these, and even now He felt their smart. His Father's hand must smite Him, and from the en-

16*

joyment of His love He must for a time be cut off. This was the dread penalty He must endure, and it was this which

"Made the sacred drops of anguish fall "—

and drew such importunate cries from His lips. Think of this, O my soul! and learn to hate those sins which placed a gulf between even the soul of the holy Jesus and that Father whom He so loved.

But deep as was the agony of Jesus, it sealed not up His lips, nor prevented the access of His spirit to God. He still embraced the Hand which smote Him. The storm was severe, but still His simple, confiding, and child-like faith pointed to His Father in heaven. His God had said, "He would hold His hand;" and now that the deep waters have come into His soul, and He sinks where there is no standing, He pleads and rests upon the promise. It is deeply affecting to contemplate the soul of man struggling amid the storms of life to reach upward towards God, the source of its strength. How much more so to contemplate the struggles of His soul, who, single-handed and alone, had to grapple with all our foes, and to stand beneath all our accumulated sorrows. And yet our Saviour failed not: no, He prayed " more fervently." The storm was loud, but His voice was louder than the storm;

His anguish was great, but His prayers were greater. Oh, reader, what an example to thee amid the battle of life, the temptations of Satan, the sophistries of reason, the mysteries of providence, and the dark shadows of the grave, to pray on and on, and still more fervently; the darker the night, the heavier the cross! This will help us to stand in the trying day, to hope against hope, to battle with all our foes; and however rudely the winds of trial, and temptation, and affliction may blow, will keep us from making shipwreck of faith amid the storms of life.

The Traitor's Kiss.

" But Jesus said unto him, Judas, betrayest thou the Son of man with a kiss?"—Luke xxii. 48.

WITH what a holy calm and divine serenity does Christ go forth to meet the traitor who was to betray Him into the hands of sinners; with what a sweet and holy dignity from the knee of prayer does He now gird himself for the terrible conflict!

The very atmosphere of heaven and peace seems to clothe Him; already His dreadful an-

guish had pressed blood from His pores, and weak
and exhausted He goes on His way to meet the
men whom He knew were seeking His life, and,
self-possessed and unmoved, He fronts His foes.
The traitor's kiss excites no anger nor surprise;
in meek and lowly grandeur He simply says:
"Judas, betrayest thou the Son of man with a
kiss?". And yet, oh what a heart that kiss betrayed! Judas had seen the bright unveiling of
His face whom he thus betrayed; he had beheld
His glory as of the only begotten of the Father,
full of grace and truth; he had witnessed His
miracles, heard the words of wisdom which fell
from his lips, followed Him into the charmed
circle of private life, and seen His mild glory
there; and yet he could sell Him for thirty
pieces of silver, and hand Him over to death with
a kiss! Surely, if ever hypocrisy was incarnate,
and cruelty and insensibilty ever surpassed themselves in utmost wickedness, it was when a disciple's kiss handed over immaculate purity to a
felon's death—and yet this kiss excites no start
of horror, no elaborate comment from the lips of
love. And it was well: Christ left the thing to
preach itself; He knew that myriads of loving
hearts would shrink from it if He did not; that
the thing itself was its own execration. It wanted
not His words to seal its character on the page
of time: it had impressed itself never to be
effaced. Judas may weep and shed his blood,

but still the kiss remains, a scar upon the face of this world's fame, never to be removed;—a dark, deep, awful blot upon its vaunted purity and virtue;—a witness of the state of man left to himself, and of the desperate wickedness of the human heart.

Strange that the lips of purity should be thus defiled. Satan himself might well have blushed to witness such a deed, and all hell have shrieked an execration; but Jesus simply says, "Betrayest thou the Son of man with a kiss?" Ah, there were deeper wounds within than it could make; and deeper to be made. The traitor's kiss could scarcely turn the skin; deep sorrow had already seized His heart, and there was scarcely room for more. The man whose body is stretched upon a rack, will hardly mark an insect's sting. And perhaps, dear reader, were some heavy sorrow now to roll upon thy soul, thou then wouldst see that thou hadst made too much of passing grief. Bethink thee of thy Saviour's heavy heart, and learn to bear the lighter ills of life unmoved. And should thy wrongs be great, fret not thyself in any wise to do evil; remember thy Saviour and the traitor's kiss, and leave the bad deeds of thy foes to proclaim themselves, and God shall vindicate thy name. The kiss of Judas was the foil of Jesus's love; and evil words and deeds shall but beget thee fame if thou wilt strive to imitate thy Lord. But why have we dwelt upon the traitor's kiss?—to hold him up to scorn? Oh, no; he was a man, we are not more; he followed Jesus, so may we; he listened to Jesus, so may we; he prayed with Jesus, so may we; professed to love Jesus, so may we: but he betrayed Jesus, so may we. Let, then, the traitor's kiss admonish us; and, while we much profess with the lip, let us pray to God for a honest heart, and to keep us from ourselves and our foes.

The False Charge.

" And they began to accuse him, saying, We found this fellow perverting the nation, and forbidding to give tribute to Cæsar, saying that he himself is Christ a King."—Luke xxiii. 2.

WHEN the heart of man has determined upon a crime, it will ever furnish him with sophistries wherewith to justify its perpetration. The Pharisees desired to get rid of Christ; and the enmity from which the desire sprang, found plenty of reasons why He ought to die. And if the heart of man was bad enough to originate these, what is there that it will not produce? It is not sufficient that Jesus die simply; the malice of the false religionists of His day must have more. The very

name of Christ must be a bye-word and reproach.
He must be made an execration and a curse.
He must be numbered with transgressors and die
a felon's death. He who never sinned must die
as a sinner; He who embodied His father's law in
his heart and life, must perish as a lawless one.
He vindicated the truth from the false glosses of
the Pharisees; and they declared He had perverted the nation. He said, "'Render to Cæsar
the things that are Cæsar's;" and they declared
He had instructed the people to withhold tribute
from Cæsar. He had fled from the people when
they would have taken Him by force and made
Him a king; yet they affirmed that He sought to
subvert the throne of the Roman Emperor. By
these falsehoods they sought to build a slaughter-
house for God's Son : to bring His spotless lamb
to the knife, that they might gaze upon His
agonies and death. O foolish men! their moral
abattoir still remains, a monument of their perfidy;
but their victim has escaped, and the crown of
moral turpitude with which they sought to encircle
His head, for ever rests upon their own. But why
this hatred of goodness, purity, and love? Why
these savage efforts to crucify their king? Why
this exposure of their malice, even in the eyes of
a stranger and a foe? Jesus had told them the
truth; He had exposed their hypocrisy, and
humbled their pride. This could not be forgiven. Light reached them from heaven; but

their deeds were evil, and they hated it because
it made them manifest. They were not willing
to believe, because they must forsake their sins.
They must cease to be the heroes of the people,
and worship God. Yea, the despised Nazarene
Himself: rather than be judged of God, they will
judge Him; rather than condemn themselves,
they will condemn Him. And hence, oh hideous
perversion of reason and justice! these men,
clothed in sin, hypocrisy, and crime, will drag
God to their bar, and declare that Goodness itself
is not fit to live! Ah! and how often has the
Son of God thus been made to stand a trembling
culprit before the bar of human reason; while
prejudice and pride, unwilling to receive or understand His words through love of sin, have perverted His doctrines, and declared that as an
impostor and a knave He ought to die. O reader!
take heed that you emulate not the conduct of
these Jews; and before you pronounce your
verdict on the Son of God, see to it that it is
built upon truth and righteousness, and a fair
examination of his deeds and words. Should ye
be found, like those of old, who sought to brand
His name with infamy without a cause, except
that which is furnished by your own prejudice,
ignorance, and enmity, be assured of this, that
God will one day call you to a terrible account,
· and bring upon thy head a retribution as terrible
as it is righteous. God may permit thee to go on

for many years, heaping false accusations on the head of His Son; but the day will come when He will vindicate His holiness to thy everlasting confusion. Pause, then; cease to revile, and let not thy prejudice urge thee on to ruin; think, examine, pray.

But Jesus was not moved by the false accusation of those who were seeking His life. He calmly admitted what was true; He declared He *was* a King, though not in the sense His adversaries affirmed. He was the faithful and true witness, and would make known the truth though its proclamation cost Him His life. He was prepared • to seal His testimony with His blood. The truth with Him was not a common thing; it was His meat and His drink, His joy and His crown. Men may falsely accuse Him, threaten, persecute, revile, and exhaust their ingenuity to torture and destroy Him; but still truth shall dwell in His heart, indite His words, and shine in His life. Mountains of sorrow may be cast upon His soul, but they shall not press error from His lips, nor cause His mind to embrace a lie. What an example to us! May we never be ashamed of the truth, but in the face of all opposition, cost us what it may, let us hold it fast, and seek to make it known! May we think of Him who has bequeathed it to us, a precious legacy sealed with His blood, and rather die than permit it to be plucked from our grasp. But let us not forget,

17

that, if thus we are helped to cleave to Christ, reproach and misrepresentation may come upon us even as they did upon Him; and let us strive to learn in patience to commit our cause to God.

The Parted Garments.

"And when they had crucified him, they parted his garments, casting lots upon them, what every man should take."—
.Mark xv. 24.

MANY precious things have been torn asunder by the rude hand of ignorance and cruelty, over which both science and art have sorely wept: but there are few things, the destruction of which has caused more sorrow to some, than that of the sacred vesture of the Son of God. And yet it was well it should be so, for many might have worshipped the robe, who would have despised the wearer; and such is the spirit of Rome. She will exhibit the clothing of Christ, but not Christ Himself. She will hold up the crown of thorns, but not His sacred temples—the spear which pierced Him, but not His bleeding heart. Over His garments she will weep, but not over His torn and bleeding body. It was a crime with her to separate His robe, but none to separate His words.

His external man shall appear, but the inner glory must be veiled. She will make a sacred drama of His death, and seek to act out the dread scene afresh; but the great truths it embodies she neither perceives herself, nor will she permit them to be exhibited to others. O proud, pretentious, but ignorant church! like the rude soldiery, thou wilt receive the clothes of Christ, but deny His words; thou wilt part His garments among thy children, but keep back the truth by which alone they can be made free.

The temporal and fading, O vain harlot! thou wilt grasp, but the spiritual and enduring has no value in thy eyes. To gaze upon the relics of the Saviour thou wilt travel many miles; but thou wilt not look at Him as He stands by thy side, exhibiting His glory to the eye of faith. His garments thou wilt receive, seeking to make money by His apparel, while the doctrines He proclaimed thou hearest but to despise. Oh, how many follow thy example, and profess Christ for a crust, while they spurn His cross, and view His word but as the duplicates of pence! How many cleave to the outward form, to the extrinsics of a living Christ, to the exclusion of the spiritual life, and miserably perish, grasping the mere symbols through which it was intended to flow.

" *And the soldiers parted his garments.*" Well, Rome will weep over these; but let the believer reserve his tears for a divided church and the fair

body of truth so frequently torn and mangled, not
only by the proud and unhumbled, but by those
whose work it is to maintain its unity and strength.
And with our tears let us blend our earnest
prayer, that the wounds of Zion may be speedily
healed, and soon before the eyes of the world but
one fold may appear, even as there is but one
Shepherd.

"*And they parted his garments.*"   Our Saviour
had not much to leave ; how affectingly His poverty appears at His death.   It was but His garments the soldiers *could* divide : there was nothing
more.   They might have been woven by the
fingers of love, but they were all that He had.
They had covered His sacred body through many
a weary journey, but they will not be wanted
again.   And it may be, believer, that thou hast
reached the end of life's journey, with little else
than the clothes that cover thee.   Thou hast
worked hard, it may be, but this is all thou hast—
a scanty wardrobe well soiled by many a hard
day's toil.   A will thou needest not make, for
thou hast nothing to leave.   Well, it was so with
thy Lord.

Thou art as rich as He was, and hast as much to
leave.   He worked as hard as thou hast, and
shed more tears, both by night and day ; so thou
canst not complain, nor from thy poverty draw
an argument against the love of thy God.   Yea,
it is possible that the garments the soldiers parted

were received from the hand of charity; and so, perhaps, are thine; so that thy poverty does but furnish thee, after all, with another feature of resemblance to thy Lord. But think not of the poor clothing which now covers thee, and which thou must soon leave behind, but of the shining raiment thou art speedily to receive from the hand of Him who, though He was rich, yet for thy sake became poor, that we through His poverty might be made rich; who wandered here in nakedness and sorrow, a forlorn outcast, that we might reach a mansion of bliss and be clothed in a robe of righteousness, by which we should be qualified for the very presence of God, and the enjoyment of His love for ever.

The Scourge.

"And when he had scourged Jesus, he delivered him to be crucified."—Matt. xxvii. 26.

How clearly did our Saviour perceive every element in that bitter cup of suffering and sorrow which our sins placed in His hands to drink! Long before the whip tore and lacerated His back He referred to it, and said, "Behold, we go up to Jerusalem, and the Son of man shall be betrayed

17*

unto the chief priests, and unto the scribes, and
they shall condemn him to death, and shall de-
liver him to the Gentiles, to mock, and to scourge,
and to crucify Him." And the Jews themselves
own to the eternal obloquy and shame which this
act entails, in the following words :—" And the
elders of Jerusalem took Jesus and brought him
to the city, and bound him to a marble pillar in
the city, *and smote him with whips, or whipped
him ;* and said unto him, Where are all thy
miracles which thou hast done ?" Poor benighted
Jew, how strangely didst thou forget the words
of thy own prophet which declared, that thy
Messiah should be " a man of sorrows and acquainted with grief ;" that " he should be led as
a lamb to the slaughter ; that the chastisement
of thy peace was to be upon him, and that by his
stripes thou wert to be healed." Ah ! little
thought our Saviour's tormentors that His weeping back proclaimed their blindness. The Son
of God bound to a marble pillar !—whipped !
Well might the stone have wept at such indig-
nity, have blushed beneath the purple tide those
cruel thongs drew forth. , O wondrous love !
which led the Saviour thus to give His back to
the smiters, and His cheeks to those who plucked
off the hair ! Mark now, believer, and see that
patient Man, gored by the savage whip—He
shrinks not, He utters no murmuring word : 'tis
but the beginning of His sacred woe,—there are

wounds even now more deeply ploughed upon
His soul, through which the burning wrath of
God must run to quench itself in agony more
deep. Yet not in fury shall that tide flow forth,
but in righteousness, to spare the lost. And shall
we faint beneath the strokes of love, or fly the
chastisement which seeks our peace? A scourged
Saviour holds the rod the strokes of which oft
make us droop our heads. He has no pleasure in
our tears, but seeks to drive us from those sins
which tore His flesh and gave him to the hands
of cruel men. And let us not forget that in this
world the Saviour still is scourged. Bound hand
and foot, He scarcely can be heard for mocking
tongues. To the cold marble column of philosophy, so called, oft found in colleges and
schools, Reason has often tied Him, while the
learned rabble and unbelieving herd have put
their thoughts together to form a thong with
which to whip His life away. One central spot
of scorn the world has known in every age—a
scourged Saviour. Still does the cold critic
weave his words to bite His flesh, and still it
seems to yield in quivering impotence. Ah!
but the scourged Man one day will show
His strength, nor yield His back to infamy for
ever; and for each subtle thought and lying
word, which brought a cord to bind or scourge
His truth, will He bring men to judgment. And
thou, too, Respectability! that often scourged

Him, by polite and gentle usage—who would have His words kept back, and thoughts attenuated by the rack of carnal policy—even thou shalt one day find the hand of Christ too strong upon thee, and the despised Nazarene shall reward thee according to thy deeds. Oh that we may seek earnestly for grace, that so neither by our words nor deeds we may be left to scourge the Saviour again, or put Him to an open shame!

The Scarlet Robe.

" And they stripped him, and put on him a scarlet robe."—
Matt. xxvii. 28.

THEY would make their derision to be notorious, and cover Christ with the most flagrant shame. To this end they took from Him what was His own, and gave to Him what did not belong to Him. And how frequently have we done the same; withholding from Him the homage due to His name, and putting Him to shame by our lives. We now execrate the conduct of those who thus mocked the Son of God; but have we not done worse? They put upon Him a scarlet robe: our sins baptized Him in His blood. How naked would our souls have been had not the body of Christ been thus clothed in the garb of apparent infamy and death! He deserved not the shame which they would fain have put upon Him; and had He not robed Himself in our nature that He might bring us shining raiment from heaven, the scarlet robe had never been His. He clothed the heavens in light as a garment, the earth in beauty and joy, and men's souls with purity and righteousness; while yet, when He appeared below, all that the world could afford Him was a vesture of scorn and reproach.

The Crown of Thorns.

" And when they had platted a crown of thorns, they put it upon his head, and a reed in his right hand: and they bowed the knee before him, and mocked him, saying, Hail, King of the Jews !"—Matt. xxvii. 29.

AND King of the Jews He was, and never more glorious than now, notwithstanding the scarlet robe and crown of thorns they had placed upon Him. He stands now before them the King of the curse, although *they* perceived it not. It was meet and right that He who was made a curse for us, who came to absorb all its bitter elements in Himself, should be crowned with thorns. Well

did they symbolise our sins, and the piercing
wounds they give. Place them, too, on His head,
and let them form a crown, for still He *is* a King,
although despised. The thorns, too, on his brow
will blossom into bliss, and yield sweet fruit. No
other way can Nature lose her stings. Oh, fruitful soil of Jesus' temples, that even thorns can
flourish there, and yield sweet honey to the soul!
Strange that the Son of God should be thus
crowned; but what else could man bring, himself
a thorn? Oh, coronation-day of heaven's own
King!—how poor this world to yield Thee nought
but thorns! It brought *its own*, and Thou in
love didst take and wear its scornful gift, to hide
its poverty and bear its griefs away. The curse
enwrapped around thy sacred head—Ah, yes!
and even from Thy feet it spread, but spread itself
to die, to perish; for Thou shalt live and never
die. 'Twas meet that they should bring Thee
thorns who made the curse. In heaven, O Lord,
Thou hadst no thorns; it was from this world
that Thou wouldst pluck the chaplet of Thy griefs,
and by the circle of Thy sorrows for ever· rob
Thy Church of all her woes. Who ever saw so
fair a head, despite the weighty burden of its
wounds? Thorns, thorns; ah! what but thorns
could clasp His temples in this world where all
had sinned? But see they spring forth into fame,
and for His thorns this King shall reign, and live
enthroned in wounded hearts for evermore. All

hail, despised King! Thy crown shall flourish
when all others fade. Faith sees Thy head no
more in sorrow bowed, but, far above the clouds
of time, the thorns all gone, transformed into a
starry crown of bliss, and feels the hand of Mercy
place upon her head while gazing thus, a circlet,
too, of joy, lined with the costly ermine of a
Saviour's love, and weeps and sings His praise
who were a crown of thorns.

O wondrous crown! each piercing thorn points
to Thy inmost love, Thou Saviour of the lost! No
other head was ever adorned like Thine. The
sacred beauty of Thy face abides, the awful majesty
of Thy kingly brow can suffer no eclipse, though
weighed down by grief. No barbaric pomp, nor
gold, nor precious stones, could bring to the sacred
arches of Thy thought one single ray of glory.
And where, too, are the crowned monarchs of the
earth? The world perceives them not; but, lo!
amid the wrecks of time, one King appears! His
thorny chaplet drinks the light of heaven, and
men of every age, kingdom, and tongue bow down
and worship. O marvellous crown! divine supremacy! O sacred head! that pillared up the
weight of human guilt, and while it held it up to
view put it away. For ever dear to us, then, be
this crown of thorns; and amid the pomp and
pageantry of life, the passing blaze of human
glory, oh may the sacred head of Christ appear to
pale its fires, and may we never forget those sacred

griefs which bought our freedom from the dreadful curse!

The Weary Journey.

*"And he bearing his cross went forth into a place called
the place of a skull, which is called in the Hebrew Golgotha."*
—John xix. 17.

WHAT a panorama of divine love is the life of
Christ! each scene becoming more touching, more
pregnant with sorrow, to the closing one, present-
ing us with His death.   Our Saviour had been a
cross-bearer from his earliest youth.   From the
first dawn of reason, His clear perception of what
man was, and of what He came to do and to bear,
must have placed a load of sorrow upon His heart,
such as was never carried and never could have
been borne by any one but himself.   But now, in
addition to this secret cross upon His weary
spirit, there is also another, placed by cruel men
upon IIis back.   It is not sufficient that IIis heart
labours with its grief and the heavy hand of justice pressing down His spirit, His body also must
have its load; and how affecting to the eye of
faith thus to contemplate him staggering on beneath His heavy cross, lone and sad, in the midst

of that infuriated throng! No hand of friendship ministers to His woes, no voice of love cheers His heart. His had been a weary journey for many years, and His path had grown more rugged as it approached the Golgotha of His griefs; and yet no murmuring word escaped Him. His was a solitary path at all times, but especially was it so now. The swelling tide of His sorrow is now rising too high for any human being to accompany Him. A desert had spread around Him from His earliest days, but it now grows more bleak and bare, and it was needful that it should be so, or our wilderness would never have rejoiced and blossomed as the rose. In hunger and nakedness, in weariness and watching, in loneliness and desolation, He came to identify Himself with His own. Of His people of old it was recorded, that they " wandered in the wilderness in a solitary way; they found no city to dwell in; hungry and thirsty, their soul fainted in them."

And with this path many of His children are familiar now. Is it so with thee, reader? And art thou ready to say, " that thy way is hidden from the Lord?" Look at thy Saviour; mark His weary steps, as He staggers on in the midst of cruelty and scorn, faint and weary, beneath the heavy load of thy guilt. Think of His love, purity, and obedience. Yet mark His path: might not He have concluded that truly He was

18

forsaken, and that His God and Father had for
gotten to be gracious? Oh, how weary must He
have been in heart, in head, in hands and feet;
His back torn to pieces by the whip; His ears
filled with the cruel mockings of His foes; His
friends far from Him; and a horrible death beneath the hidings of His Father's face near at
hand! Oh, what a path was His! Say now,
believer, let thy sorrowful heart have full vent;
repeat thou all thy griefs, and try if thou canst
make thy path like His. Is thy body wearied as
was His—thy hands and feet? Does thy heart
and head ache as did His? Is thy body goaded
and torn, and filled with pain as was His? Art
thou forsaken of thy friends as He was? Hast
thou as heavy a cross upon thy back? Is thy
character slandered as was His? Are thy ears
as filled with the yells of cruelty, and the voices
of those who are about to take thy life? Hast
thou the prospect of the same death. Great as
may be thy afflictions, wilt thou not admit, that
to compare them with the sufferings of Christ
were sacrilege indeed? Thy path, it may be, is
rugged; but in thy darkest night hast thou not
the star of hope?

Thy cross *is* heavy; but hast thou not a mighty
Saviour upon whom thou canst lean, and who invites thee ever to find peace and rest in His love?
Hast thou not His precious words to gird thee
with strength? and, however solitary thy path,

hast thou not the promise of His presence, and the whispers of His love through the sacred ministrations of His Divine Spirit? Oh, how rich art thou in all the extremities of thy grief compared with thy Lord! Oh! lose not thy peace, the quiet and rest of thy spirit, by looking too much to thy trouble; by fixing thy eyes upon the briars and thorns of thy way. But let thy faith stedfastly eye Him who—with His chaplet of thorns, His bleeding back, His weary feet, and wounded, fainting spirit—still meekly and silently, and without a murmuring word, amid blasphemy and contempt, moved on to the accomplishment of that death by which thy sins were to be expiated—thy soul redeemed—a cordial of love prepared for all thy sorrows—and a right and title to a mansion of bliss and a crown of glory which fadeth not away. Thus musing upon the sorrows of Jesus, thou shalt forget thy own, and receive from Him that grace which shall rob them of their sting, and enable thee to pluck from them occasions for present and everlasting praise.

.

The Cruel Death.

"And they crucified him."—Mark xv. 25.

THE weary steps of Christ at length came to
a pause; but it was at the brink of the grave—
a shameful and ignominious death. At length,
through scenes of manifold temptations, sufferings, and sorrows, He has reached the dreadful
goal to which, with the undying constancy of
love, He has pressed on from His very birth, and
where He will bring to a glorious consummation
the great work which His Father gave him to do,
and which was to ensure the undying bliss of the
myriads He came to redeem.

   " And there they crucified him."—The meek and
lowly Man who permitted them to place the cross
upon His back, permitted them also to stretch
His hands and feet upon it, and with the hammer
and rugged nails to fix them there. O mysterious love! O meek yet Almighty Saviour! how
was it that no ray of thy Godhead escaped in the
midst of such cruelty, to wither and to blast for
ever the wicked hands which sought Thy death?
O wondrous love! which held Thy power in
check, and kept Thee passive as a lamb beneath
the wounds which drained Thy life away! O

holiness! how dear wast thou to the heart of
Jesus! Rather than see thy garments stained by
sin, He gives His blood! O justice! how precious to the Lamb of God wast thou! Rather
than thou shouldst waive thy righteous claims,
unholy men shall nail His body to the tree; and
inch by inch He will die; and calmly, slowly,
'mid sweat, and wounds, and blood, and darkness,
and agonies unutterable, and death, He will pay
into thy hands the utmost which thy law demands. And thou, too, Mercy, how closely to
the heart of Jesus didst thou cleave; rather than
part with thee, His heart shall bleed, that with
the purple tide thy hand might blend a balm to
heal the wounds of men.

"*And there they crucified Him.*"—To this end,
earth and hell had watched Him from the cradle
to the grave. They had hung upon His steps
like dogs; they had followed Him, and at last
enclosed Him. They came nearer and nearer
until they put their savage hands upon Him, and
with yells of fury sought His destruction. It was
a lingering and awful death Christ died. His
bodily pains no words can reach. He could say,
"I am poured out like water, and all my bones
are out of joint; my heart is like wax; it is
melted in the midst of my bowels. My strength
is dried up like a potsherd; and my tongue
cleaveth to my jaws; and thou hast brought me
into the dust of death." Through His great pain

18*

and anguish of mind, a burning fever seized upon Him, and made Him exclaim, I "thirst!" This speedily robbed Him of His strength and His flesh, so that casting a sorrowful look upon His emaciated body, He exclaimed, "I may tell all my bones: they look and stare upon me!" Well might He exclaim to His God, "But be not thou far from me, O Lord: O, my strength, haste thee to help me!"

But, after all, the pains of our Redeemer were not mere bodily pains. There was a cross upon which the mind was stretched as well as the body. The sensibilities of His body were great; but those of His soul were greater. To what extent the soul of man is capacitated for suffering, is a dread secret never fully realized in this world; though sometimes, from the trouble and anguish produced when but a few drops of Divine wrath fall upon it, we may form some little idea. In this respect, all the powers of Christ's soul were peculiarly sensitive; and, upheld and supported by His Divine nature, no doubt they could, and did, drink in an amount of anguish beyond all human or angelic comprehension. The hand of God, as a righteous judge, brought all the elements of the penalty attached to sin into His experience; and in suffering and sorrow He exhausted them all. And He *could* exhaust them; for, while His nature was finite, it was no less infinite. To what extent the soul can suffer,

who can say? but as united to the Divine nature,
who will dare to declare? From the mouth of '
His servant David we learn that He sank in deep
waters where there was *no standing;* that the
wrath of God lay *hard* upon Him; "and thou,"
said He, "hast afflicted me with *all thy waves.*"
Both the superior and inferior natures were both
engaged in that last terrible conflict of the Redeemer, by which the sins of His people were at
once and for ever expiated, and the power of hell
overthrown. Let us ever approach the conflict
with holy awe. Let us ever gaze with love and
reverence upon those sorrows by which our griefs
are healed; and may the simple statements of the
Word of God ever be the resting-place of our
faith. He who has felt but a little of the terrors
of God's law, and of the hidings of God's face,
will ever look with profound reverence upon the
travail of His soul, who stood solitary and alone
in the midst of penal darkness, to endure in body
and soul the utmost penalty of that holy law
which has righteously consigned myriads to a retribution which stretches itself through the countless ages which are past, and into countless ages
which are yet to come.

But why must Jesus die? His death was a
matter of Divine purpose. Long before He came
into this world, He had declared by the mouth of
the inspired Psalmist, "A body hast thou prepared
me. In the volume of the book it is written of me,

I delight to do thy will, yea, thy law is within my heart." The Divine Father perceiving, from the most distant ages of eternity, how all His creatures would sin and break His law, thus exposing themselves to its penalty, determined to spoil the designs of Satan, and to save a number which no man can number, by sending His Son to bear the punishment due to their sins. Jesus also voluntarily became the surety of those whom the Father purposed to save; and hence, speaking to His Father, in His intercessory prayer, He says, "Thine they were, and thou gavest them to me." It being, therefore, a matter of Divine purpose, that the people of God should be saved by the substitution and vicarious death of the Son of God, the Divine mystery was set forth in the prophetic page. The prophets were employed by the Spirit of God to portray the glory of that Saviour, who was to come, "a light to lighten the Gentiles, and the glory of His people Israel." A suffering Saviour was the centre object of all their representations; and hence, Jesus must die in fulfilment of the word.

The attributes of God also demanded it. The people of God had by their own sins, in common with others, exposed themselves to the penalty of the law, that penalty being *righteous;* and that the justice of God might not become a common thing in the universe, it must have been endured by them or some one else. Christ came to bear it, and did bear it, so that the sinner can escape while yet righteousness is exalted, both in God and in the sinner's heart. In God, inasmuch as He receives, at the hands of Christ, a satisfaction for sin which no creature could have given; while the sinner, perceiving the inflexibility of law in the sufferings of Christ, learns to revere the justice of God, while He exults in the love which provides a ransom for his soul. On these grounds we have the recorded fact of our Saviour's death. No finite hand could have touched Him, but for the fulfilment of these gracious designs.

"*And they crucified Him.*"—An awful blot is this upon the page of the world's history, an everlasting stain upon its pride; and well for thee, my soul, that thou shouldst cease to embrace a world, whose archives are thus defiled. Yet, in this fact, our hope of pardon, and peace, and purity, and heaven, has its birth. And hence the Christian must ever love to contemplate the crucified One. Jesus on the cross, the cross of Christ, a theme for present and for future bliss. The spot most sacred to the renewed heart. The home where all the Christian graces dwell and thrive. The meeting place of God and man. The mirror of God's love. The apocalypse of all His perfections, united in the most sweet and exalted harmony for the salvation of men. The point where all the rays of truth most brilliantly converge to show how sin can be put away, the soul be renewed, and more than paradise be re-gained. Here God's most sacred thoughts and choicest forms of wisdom show themselves to instruct and bless mankind. To this point, the returning wanderer turns his eye, and here the weary heart finds rest. Here all heaven's richest blessings grow in clusters, and Omnipotence reaches forth its hand, through frailty, to save and elevate the lost.

In the wounds of Jesus faith discovers the honey of God's love, and learns a secret hidden from the wise. The dove of peace dwells here, perpetually shedding, from its outstretched wings, the dew of heaven to fertilize the barren mind. Here Mercy gathers all her children to heal their wounds, to teach them the lessons of eternal love, as they are written on the broken body of her bleeding Lord; and the first notes of that ever-lasting hymn the redeemed shall sing for ever-more. Here death, too, loses its sting, and hell its prey. Here to the eye of faith light breaks forth brighter than the sun, with healing on its wings: a light which pales all human glory, and spreads and flies, and flies and spreads, until the entire universe, bathed in heaven's own beauty, reflects the praise of God. O Cross of Christ! the sun, the moon, and stars, the flowers, the trees, the fields, in one perpetual hymn tell much —but thou, infinitely more! No other world has known thy charms; grasped by the hand of

Love, thou touchest this, and dost transmute its base alloy to gold. The pall of sorrow death has thrown upon it: as it sighs and moans along its silent way, a gloomy sepulchre, thou dost remove, and clothe it in the garments of perpetual joy, the bridal raiment of a king. The dark enigmas reason cannot solve, thou makest plain. The long sad night of sorrow at thy presence leaves the earth, which, now transformed like some pellucid sea, so brightly shines, that angels, as they fly, look down and see themselves reflected from beneath, and gaze upon the very smile of God. The church through thee shall wear a beauty which shall never die; and nature, too, shall hear the voice of God, and hearing shall obey, and learn the mighty meaning of those words, " Behold, I make all things new."

Sad day, then, for this world, when men by misty statements hide the cross—the Church's hope, and burden of her bliss; the perennial fountain of her joy, her purity, and peace. Dark is the night that soon will overshadow us; the sweet dove of peace will soon withdraw, and universal discord reign. Let but the tidings of a Saviour's death cease to be proclaimed, and universal death will speedily seize us all. Let His broken body be but entombed in human speculations, or philosophic pride, and soon the melting, fertilizing rays of heaven's own sun will cease to shine, and moral desolation spread on all around;

the barren winter of worldliness, selfishness, and
pride will reign; the arid sands of human speculation encompass all—a dreary waste over which
the aching eye seeks often for the footsteps of
eternal love, but finds them not; and where the
weary, thirsty heart cries out in vain for the living waters of revealed truth, and in despair at
last lies down to die.

Oh, then, my soul, dwell near the cross; and
while others wander over the classic page, or seek
an hiding-place beneath the spreading branches of
scholastic lore, or art, or taste, make this thy joy!
View every form of truth and beauty as thy friend;
but let the cross of Jesus be thy home; here dwell,
thou sublimely lost, yet truly found; and let the
truths which grow and cluster here, be ever to thee
the sweet, the sacred ambrosia of thy soul, and
live to make them known.

Reader, come to the cross—the culminating
point of this world's sorrows, it is true; still, if
thou wilt but come, it shall not be to thee a
gloomy place. Here thou shalt find happiness
like a star upon the brow of night; and while
gazing upon the death of Jesus, the bloom and
freshness of immortal youth shall come upon thee.
From His precious blood thy faith shall fetch in
pardon for all thy sins, and gather honey from
the flower of hope, which blossoms here, and
never fades. The holy fragrance of Almighty
love will steep thy heart in bliss. Here the Spirit

of God will meet with thee, and claim affinity again with thy spirit, and dwell with thee a fountain of wisdom and perpetual peace. Here all thy powers shall be harmonised, and thy self-will shall be slain ;—

"The life-long bleeding of the heart be o'er."

For it shall beat responsive to God's love, and thy will shall move in accordance with the eternal law of happiness and peace. Wrong not, then, thy spirit, reader, of its balm and rest. Come to love's sanctuary for the weary. Consent thou to be blessed. Let thy soul become the temple of Jesus, thy heart His throne, then shall thy life become a book of wonders; thy lips an oracle of truth; thy tongue an instrument whose melody heaven shall approve; thy intellect the palace of its king; while thy memory shall be inlaid with the most costly tokens of God's love; and, thus beautified and blessed, thou shalt embody and exhibit diviner mysteries, and more of God than all the universe besides, and commence a jubilee of joy and never-ending praise.

"Him on yonder cross I love,
Nought on earth I else count dear.
May He mine for ever prove
Who is now so inly near.
Here I stand; whate'er may come,
Days of sunshine or of gloom,
From this word I will not move;
Him upon the cross I love!

19

'Tis not hidden from my heart,
    What true love must often bring;
Want and grief have sorest smart,
    Care and scorn can sharply sting.
Nay, but if Thy will were such,
Bitterest death were not too much.
Dark though here my course may prove,
Him upon the cross I love!

Rather sorrows such as these,
    Rather love's acutest pain,
Than without Him days of ease,
    Riches false and honours vain.
Count me strange when I am true,
What He hates I will not do;
Sneers no more my heart can move;
Him upon the cross I love!

Know ye whence my strength is drawn,
    Fearless thus the fight to wage?
Why my heart can laugh to scorn
    Fleshly weakness, Satan's rage?
'Tis, I know the love of Christ;
Mighty is that love unpriced.
What can grieve me, what can move?
Him upon the cross I love!

Once the eyes that now are dim
    Shall discern the changeless love,
That hath led us home to Him,
    That hath crown'd us far above.
Would to God that all below
What that love is now might know,
And their hearts this word approve:
Him upon the cross I love!"

                    GREDING. (Born 1676.)
                    Lyra Germanica.

"To God's blessing upon the bold and faithful assertion of such noble truths as election, justification, sanctification, and perseverance, we owe our reformation from Popery. So nothing will finally preserve us from being carried captive into the Popish Egypt again, but the revival and preaching of those same noble truths."—LUTHER.

"Each day brings its trials; but their bitterness passes away, while the sweetness of its blessings remains, like the rose scent in the vase. The unnumbered kindnesses of God, the countless small pleasures which mark His unslumbering thoughtfulness for us, are like bright ears of corn scattered along our path to tell us of the golden harvest-field from whence they come, and towards which we are journeying; crystal drops from the river of life, which maketh glad the city of God. Such things cheer us on in this earth, but should not bind us to it; rather should they send us onward with joyfulness, eager for the bliss that God has prepared for us on high, and longing for those pleasures which are at his right hand for evermore."

Man's best thoughts in times of trial are often found to be but broken cisterns, which refuse a single drop of consolation to the weary soul; but God's thoughts, like wells fed by a living spring, perpetually give forth the enlivening and refreshing streams of spiritual peace and joy.

"We cannot expect spiritual thoughts and affections from truths which are but imperfectly understood, or doubtfully and feebly believed."—J. A. JAMES, *of Birmingham.*

𝕾ells of 𝕾alvation;

OR,

THE JOY OF THE CHURCH.

"Therefore with joy shall ye draw water out of the wells of salvation."—Isa. xii. 3.

THE seraphic prophet commences his sweet gospel sonnet by directing the attention to a certain day —a period of time—"in that day," he says; " a glorious day is this, the light and splendour of which shall never decline, for Christ is its sun, a sun that shall never set, but continue to throw forth its light and beauty through the countless ages of eternity." And in connexion with this divine period the prophet also brings before us the employment of the redeemed—"In that day thou shalt *say*, O Lord, I will praise Thee," &c.

The people, it seems, shall talk; and what is easier than to use the tongue? But they shall use theirs to a good purpose: in their case it shall be their glory, and not their shame; grace shall

19*

teach their hearts and make their lips discourse sweet music; they shall talk well, for they shall be instructed; they shall not be left to say anything, or desire to speak at random; God's deeds and not their own shall form their theme; they shall give utterance to His thoughts, and not their own; they shall praise Him, and not themselves; His mercy shall be the key-note of their song, and they shall lead off every strain which arises from this sin-stricken world, having for its object, "Glory to God in the highest, and on earth peace, good will towards men."

Their song shall be *constant;* there shall be the ringing forth of an everlasting chime through every age; amid the chaos of strange sounds, the storm music of this lower world, the spiritually-educated ear shall detect it, as the soft, sweet, melodious theme which ever pervades it, giving meaning to its discords, rising and falling, but never entirely lost.

The various phases of human thought ebb and flow, different systems of philosophy rise and fall, but in the midst of the ever-floating and shifting débris of sentiment and feeling, God's thoughts shall continue. God has determined that they shall live in men's hearts, and find an intelligent utterance in their lives. Generation after generation comes and goes, but in the midst of each God ever places His sweet singers to give the key-notes to the coming ages of all that is truly good

and great. It is a simple and sublime song which
the redeemed ever sing, for it is not built upon the
theories of men, the wild vagaries of theological
dreamers, the empty conceits of doctors of divinity,
the semi-rationalistic teaching of initiative theolo-
gians, but upon the eternal and immutable WORD
OF GOD ; the truth as realised in their own living
experience, and the great things which God has
done for their salvation. And hence, notwithstanding the contempt and scorn with which these
simple and illiterate songsters are frequently
treated by the wise and prudent in their own
eyes, they continue to live, and to give utterance
to thoughts which shall live and burn, and continue to cheer and guide the living host of God's
elect over the barren sands of this wilderness, and
upwards and onwards far above the clouds of
human speculation to the very throne of God and
the Lamb.

The prophet having referred to a period, and
declared what the redeemed should say, and the
holy and divine assurance which should mark
their speech, next proceeds to make known what
they should *do*, and says, " Therefore with joy
shall ye draw water out of the wells of salvation."
We will notice these wells, and the employment
of the people of God in connexion therewith.

The wells of salvation.—It is said, that while the
French engineers were boring for water in the
African desert, the Arabs looked on in silent won-

der, until they saw the precious stream actually
gushing forth, and then their joy knew no bounds;
and sweet and precious as the cooling waters are
now to the weary, labouring child of the desert,
so precious were they to the people to whom the
words of the prophet were originally addressed;
and the promise to them of an indefinite supply
of that element which is so essential to natural
life, would be highly appreciated by them, and
well calculated to inspire their gratitude and joy.
But there can be no doubt but that these words refer
to the mind more than the body, and to spiritual
rather than natural life. And we have here a promise to the people of God, that for them there
shall ever be mediums of divine deliverance and
spiritual refreshment in the desert of time, until
the gospel day shall lose itself in the brightness
and beauty of eternity's morning.

We may apply the figure to the persons of
Deity. In the Scriptures, God the Father is ever
brought before us as the great original spring-
head, and source of salvation to His people: and
hence we find Him reproving them for "forsaking
Him, the fountain of living waters, to hew out to
themselves broken cisterns which could hold no
water."

God the Son also may be viewed as a well of
salvation. "If any man thirst," said He, "let
him come unto me, and drink;" and on another
occasion, "Whosoever shall drink of the water

which I shall give him shall never thirst; but the water that I shall give him shall be in him, a well of water springing up into everlasting life;" while the Holy Spirit is represented by the same divine Teacher, as being the medium through which these living waters flow; "for," says the inspired apostle, "the kingdom of God is not in meat nor drink, but righteousness and peace and joy in the holy Ghost."

The doctrines of divine grace may also be viewed as so many wells of salvation to the soul, for "Ye shall know the truth," said our Saviour, "and the truth shall make you free," and "Sanctify them by thy truth; thy word is truth."

1. *A covenant ordered in all things and sure.*—This eternal and immutable covenant, which has for its object the salvation of all God's people, has been a source of strong consolation to the spiritually-educated but afflicted pilgrims of Zion in every age, and hence such have been wont to say, "that it is all their salvation and all their desire." Some Christians cannot see this covenant as revealed of God; the New Testament, is, however, but an amplification of it in so many words; and as a book exists in the mind of an author before it has a visible incarnation through the medium of ink and paper, so the covenant of grace existed in the mind and purpose of God long before it had an intelligent expression in the language of men upon the sacred page.

2. *Electing love.*—This is a deep well, bringing its sweet waters from the very depths of eternity. True it is, some either through ignorance or prejudice, refuse to drink at this well; but oh, with what joy did the Apostle drink of its waters! "Blessed be the God and Father of our Lord Jesus Christ, who hath blessed us with all spiritual blessings in heavenly places in Christ, according as He hath chosen us in him before the foundation of the world, that we should be holy and without blame before Him in love." Those who are indifferent to religion, ought not to be offended by that which they practically declare does not concern them, and of which they can have no competent knowlege; while surely it should give no offence to those who love Jesus to be told, that their love to Him declares them to be the especial objects of His eternal and peculiar love.

3. *Particular redemption.*—This is a well, the flow of whose deep and crimsoned waters removes all obstructions from the path of divine mercy, as she comes forth to the help and succour of the wretched and lost. By the side of this well the redeemed have been wont to sit in every age, to muse upon the love of God, while the wonders it has accomplished ever form the theme of their most sweet and exalted song.

4. *Divine calling.*—Through this well the water of divine grace first flows into the soul. "And in that day shall the deaf hear the words of the

book, and the eyes of the blind shall see out of obscurity, and out of darkness." "Who hath saved us," says the Apostle, "and called us with an holy calling, not according to our works, but according to His own purpose and grace, which was given us in Christ Jesus before the world began."

Pardon.—This is a well much frequented by the guilty in quest of mercy; and oh! how sweet are its waters to the soul when all but fainting beneath the burning heat of divine displeasure and the burden of sin!

Justification.—This well ever yields a rich and constant supply of the deep waters of peace; "Being justified by faith, we have peace with God."

Sanctification.—"To be carnally minded is death: to be spiritually minded is life and peace." The most corrupt and depraved are cleansed by the waters of this well.

Perseverance.—"I give unto them eternal life, and they shall never perish, neither shall any pluck them out of my hand." Oh! how many of the sheep of mercy's pasture would have perished but for this well! how frequently has its reviving streams restored their drooping faith! "He restoreth my soul."

Glorification.—This may be spoken of as a well of delight to the earnest pilgrim, especially when the wilderness is cold and bleak, and yields no green thing to refresh the eye; its ever-flowing waters frequently make a paradise in the soul. Sitting by its side, the weary spirit gathers strength, the sad heart loses the burden of its sorrows, while faith wipes the tear from the eye, and points to the land of the blest.

The *precious and adapted promises of the Gospel*, also, may be viewed as so many wells of salvation to the soul; and, however barren and desolate the path of the travelling church, it is ever fringed with these wells, whose waters fail not; although, like Hagar of old, she frequently perceives them not until God opens her eyes. And hence it is written, "The wilderness and solitary place shall be glad for them; and the desert shall rejoice and blossom as the rose." Wherever the redeemed go, the river-tide of Divine mercy follows them, ever singing as it flows, to bless them and make them blessings. The promises of God never spread themselves before the eye of faith as a deceitful mirage, but as a sea of love from which the waters of peace ever flow.

The *precepts of Christ*, also, are frequently proved to be so many wells of salvation to the real Christian. Hence said the Psalmist, "I will not forget thy precepts, for by them thou hast quickened me;" and, "by the words of thy mouth have I kept myself from the paths of the destroyer."

All *the relative names and offices of Christ* are so many wells of salvation. Oh, how precious to those who know and love Him! The ordinances of God's house, when filled with His blessing, are also wells of salvation to those who are seeking the favour of the Most High. The Lord was with His disciples of old in the breaking of bread and prayer; and it was when baptized in the river Jordan, that the dove of peace descended upon the head of Christ, and the voice of His Father was heard, saying, "This is my beloved Son, in whom I am well pleased: hear ye him."

Nor should we forget that by the ordinance of secret prayer, the redeemed of the Lord have frequently opened a well in the wilderness: "who passing through the Valley of Baca, make it a well." It is this mysterious, this prevalent power of faith in the believer, which converts this wilderness into an Eden of fruitfulness and joy, and opens a river of life and peace from the bleak and barren rock of affliction, poverty, and death. Of the wells of salvation, the believer, therefore, may, ever in faith and in prayer, earnestly and constantly exclaim, "Spring up, O well!" for from these wells are destined to flow forth those streams which shall ultimately gird the entire universe with fertility and joy.

But these wells are to afford employment to the redeemed: "With joy shall ye draw water out of the wells of salvation." Through the mediums mentioned, the people of God are to receive the water of Divine grace, life, and peace; they

20

are to *draw* water. If asked, how?—by using the means God has appointed—the ordinances of God's house, secret and public prayer; but above all, by believing: faith is the simple and sublime instrumentality by which the Christian drinks of those streams which make glad the city of God. "He that believeth on me, out of his belly shall flow rivers of living water."

And for what purpose shall the redeemed draw these waters? For their own encouragement, consolation, strength, and fruitfulness; and also for the benefit of others; for "no man liveth to himself," saith the Apostle, "and no man dieth to himself; but whether we live or die, we are the Lord's." Oh, how frequently do believers seek earnestly a blessing for others, when their sense of personal unworthiness seems all but to preclude the hope that they can receive one for themselves!

But, *with joy* shall ye draw water. Why *with joy?* Because their service shall be a service of love, and love makes labour light—a *free* service: they shall serve as sons and not as slaves. Because their service shall be disinterested, and such a service is ever pleasant. Because it shall be a holy service, and such a service must be a happy service. The prophet, however, assigns the reason in the context. "And in that day thou shalt say, O Lord, I will praise thee: though thou wast angry with me, thine anger is turned away, and thou comfortest me ;" " *therefore* with joy shall ye draw water out of the wells of salvation."

" Behold, God is thy salvation !" " *therefore* with joy shall ye draw water out of the wells of salvation."

" I will trust and not be afraid ;" " *therefore* with joy shall ye draw water out of the wells of salvation."

" For the Lord Jehovah is my strength and my song; He also is become my salvation ;" " *therefore* with joy shall ye draw water out of the wells of salvation."

The reader will observe that the chief reason why the church is to draw water with joy out of the "wells of salvation," is the holy and sublime assurance she has of her interest in God—" Behold, God is my salvation !" This is the life-giving root of all true joy and spiritual service; and because God ever lives, the wells of salvation can never run dry; the church shall continue as a garden enclosed, and a living spring, whose waters fail not; " *therefore* with joy shall ye draw water out of the wells of salvation."

From the whole, then, we may learn, that although believers are very highly favoured and distinguished of God, they nevertheless continue to be spiritually poor and dependent upon their Lord; that God has provided all that they can possibly need to meet their wants, and to make them equal to a joyful and happy service; and

that it is their duty and privilege to avail themselves of what He has in love provided. We may
learn, still further, that assurance of interest in the
love of God is the root of all spiritual activity in
His service, and that the obedience He requires is
cheerful and intelligent, and a source of satisfaction
and delight to the soul; and, finally, that the doctrines of divine grace, being so many sources of
spiritual life, refreshment, and strength to the
soul, can never become obsolete, and that so far as
they are wilfully kept back, or ignorantly superseded by something else, to the same extent must
the Church lose her spiritual health, joy, and
fruitfulness. Many who have drunk but very
superficially of the wells of salvation, and who,
whatever they may know of other things, know
but little of themselves, or of Divine teaching,
speak of the growth of the church as a something
so transcendent as to have superseded the old-
fashioned wells of salvation. These are too rustic
for their approbation; but let not the believer be
deceived. Men may have more faith in their own
dreams than God's word, and prefer their own
thoughts to His; they may originate new systems
or mar God's, thinking they are doing Him service; but, after all, their thoughts and schemes
turn out to be but broken cisterns. They may
alter and modify them, elaborate, carve and gild
them—make them of gold, silver, copper, or brass:
still they are but *broken* cisterns which hold no

water, and only serve to mock the thirst of the heaven-bound pilgrim.

It is the duty and privilege of the church, therefore, to stand by the " wells of salvation;" to remember that truth is immutable and will never change; that God will conquer the world by His own thoughts, and not man's; that though the age may advance in knowledge, yet, if men are to be saved, they must come to the " wells of salvation" to drink; that sin is the same in this age, as those which have preceded it, and that God's method of putting it away is the same; that man is as unjust as ever he was, and that God has the same method of justifying him; that the heart is still as corrupt, and that God has the same grace, by which He cleanses it. Let us not, therefore, be carried away by *fine talk*, but listen to the words of Christ. " Sanctify them by thy truth," said He; " thy word is truth." The same truth which sanctified the church triumphant, is to elevate the church militant; and let us endeavour to show the reality of spiritual growth above and beyond our fathers, by the reverence we manifest for the Gospel of Christ, and by seeking to drink at the wells of pure and unadulterated truth.

Let us give heed to the apostolic admonition, " Beware lest any man spoil you through philosophy and vain deceit, after the rudiments of the world, and not after Christ." Let us remember, believer, that it is our especial vocation to make

20*

known the "wells of salvation;" and when we perceive a poor creature wearied in the greatness of his way, seeking happiness and finding none, let us direct him to the true source of peace and joy. Oh, may the Gospel become increasingly precious to us! may it be our joy to point the guilty to the well of full and free forgiveness, through a crucified Redeemer, and the tried and afflicted saint to that spring of sovereign and immutable love which will never exhaust itself! and thus employing ourselves, we shall do more to elevate and bless our fellows than mere philosophy and eloquent talk have ever accomplished, and realise for ourselves the truth of the Divine declaration—"Therefore with joy shall ye draw water out of the wells of salvation.".

> "Not lost are they whose journey lies
>   Along the world's most tangled ways;
> Nor need they faint if burning skies
>   Dry up the wells for many days;
> Nor they repine whose lot command
> A life-path through the desert sands.
>
> For, lo! the Gospel waters clear
>   Are given to their aching eyes,
> Wherein, through mist of earthly tear,
>   They yet may see the skies,
> Along whose margin spreads the strand
> That stretches to the Holy Land.
>
> We may be poor through all our days,
>   Yet gather great increase:

Our lives may lead through rugged ways,
But all their paths be peace;
And they on earth the sons of toil,
Are heirs of an immortal soil.

'Twas thus the ladder's lowest round
Rose up where, faint and weary thrown,
The Patriarch's head no pillow found
More gentle than the stone;
Yet *there* he caught the message bright
That sounded down the golden spars,
And track'd in dreams, the steps of light
That stretch'd beyond the stars;
And knew they were the shining road
That took the angels up to God."

T. K. HERVEY, Esq.
" *Lays of the Sanctuary.*"

"Two things have shone with golden light
Upon the way where I am sent:
A rich man poor in his own sight,
And a poor man rich in his content.
But a nobler thing than even these,
And shining with a light more pure,
Is a poor man kneeling on his knees,
And thanking God that he is poor."

REV. W. W. HOW, M.A.
"*Lays of the Sanctuary.*"

"Hereby many deceive their own souls: goods, lands, posses-
sions, relations, trades, with secular interest in them, are the
things whose image is drawn on their minds, and whose characters are written on their foreheads as the titles whereby they
may be known. As believers, beholding the glory of Christ in
the blessed image of the Gospel, are changed into the same
image and likeness by the Spirit of the Lord; so these persons,
beholding the beauty of the world and the things that are in it
in the cursed glass of self-love, are in their minds changed into
the same image. Hence perplexing fears, vain hopes, empty
embraces of things perishing, fruitless desires, earthly, carnal
designs, cursed self-pleasing imaginations, feeding on, and being
fed by the love of the world and self, do abide and prevail in
them. (Eph. iv. 17—20; Rom. viii. 6.) But we have not so
learned Christ."

OWEN.

The Solemn Admonition;

OR,

A LESSON FOR THE COVETOUS.

" Take heed and beware of covetousness."—Luke xii. 15.

SIN having made man a coward at heart, he is apt to raise false alarms, and frequently, through the want of wisdom, he attaches very solemn admonitions to things scarcely worthy of his attention. This is not the case, however, with the Great Teacher and man's best Friend. If a note of warning—a beware falls from His lips, we may ever view it as a beacon-light upon some hidden rock, upon which many have made shipwreck—as a floating light amid a sea of danger ; and this is pre-eminently the case in those solemn words the importance of which induces us to cite them again : " Take heed, and BEWARE of covetousness."

Of this sin we may affirm, that it is the one great sin to which men are primarily exposed ; having ceased to desire the best of all portions, God Himself, their corrupt hearts perpetually go astray after other things, which they would fain put in His place, and make to be to their hearts what He only can be. But while this sin embraces more or less all alike, both rich and poor, binding all to the bleak and barren rock of dissatisfaction and despair, but few are conscious of its influence, and very few indeed ever confess it either before God or man. The truth is, sin has made man so completely selfish, that not until the love of God loosens his affections from himself does he become aware of the number or strength of the foes by whom he is held captive. Some, too, have a difficulty in understanding what is meant by covetousness. The word of God, however, speaks of it clearly and explicitly, as inordinate desire, perpetually striving to reach a practical issue, irrespective of right or wrong or the glory of God. It is a parent sin, and never exists by itself. The covetous man will mostly be found to be a niggard; sordid, mercenary, mean, unscrupulous, cruel, and dishonest. With such features of character, such a one might certainly be viewed as the masterpiece of Satanic agency. Let us, therefore, take heed, and beware of this sin; because

1. *It estranges from God.*—This follows as a necessary result. A covetous man is perpetually putting something else in the place of God; and hence God stands at a distance from him.

Covetousness also hardens the heart, locks up

the affections, shuts up all bowels of mercy, makes men cruel, unnatural, most unlike God, who "is love," and loves to communicate Himself. A covetous man is in fact a moral petrifaction, and with such God can hold no communion.

Covetousness leads to a suspension of that Divine influence which is essential to nearness with God. The dew will not rest upon a rock; neither will God's free, loving, and beneficent Spirit dwell with the man who, under the mastery of this odious sin, lives exclusively for the gratification of himself.

Covetousness cripples confidence in God; and when confidence in God leaves the heart, communion with Him fails: the soul finds itself upon an inclined plane, and by the weight of its own selfishness gravitates further and further from God, until faith becomes a moral impossibility, and God declares, "Ephraim is joined to idols; LET HIM ALONE!" And hence covetous men are generally timid, full of doubts and fears; a spirit of bondage binds them, and they are often afraid to die, while yet too miserable to live; for, when the heart so embraces its idol as entirely to exclude God, estrangement is complete, and all kinds of misery begin to prey upon the soul.

2. *Of its insidious development.*—This sin more than all others *grows* upon men. It resembles a certain plant, which, having selected a tree, continues to creep up and entwine its fibres so closely

around it, that at last it is suffocated, and perishes
in the embrace of the parasite which its strength
had nourished and sustained.   Oh ! let us beware
of this sin, which, like a serpent, ever seeks by
degrees to coil around us, that it may sting us
down to hell.

3. *On account of its influence upon others.*—This
sin, like all others, communicates itself.   We have
heard of a certain family, the members of which
would sit together for hours in the dark on a
winter's night, rather than be at the expense of a
candle; and yet they were possessed of thousands.
Through the indulgence of this sin, the husband
may ruin the wife, and the wife the husband; the
parents their children, and the children their
parents.   Reflect, reader, how awful to be instrumental in smiting those whom we love with a
moral leprosy, which must issue in eternal death !

4. *It pre-eminently dishonours Christ, on the part
of those who profess to be his disciples.*   " He that is
joined to the Lord is one spirit."   Should the
men of the world believe this truth, what must
they think of Christ's spirit as they see it displayed
by a covetous Christian ?   Oh ! what must be the
condemnation of those who by their covetousness
are transformed into so many living, practical,
walking, speaking libels of Christ—of Him who,
" although He was rich, yet for our sakes became
poor, that we through His poverty might be made
rich ;" who parted with all that He had, and at

last gave even Himself a sacrifice for His people, that they through Him might have eternal life.

5. *It so injures the cause of Christ.*—Covetousness is like a moth fretting a garment; however costly and beautiful it may be, by degrees it will be destroyed. And thus have many Christians for a time been robbed of all their spiritual strength and beauty; while in reference to those who have not grace, covetousness has ruined its thousands. And what this sin does for the individual, it will do for a community. Covetous ministers and deacons especially hurt the cause of God, and hold back the blessing of the Most High. Let the reader read and ponder Isa. lviii. 10—12.

6. *On account of the hell to which it exposes the soul.*—Covetousness, of all sins, most assimilates to Satan; his heart is a covetous heart, his desires are inordinate, but they all terminate in himself, irrespective of the glory of God; and hence the misery of this great but fallen spirit. The dew of God's holy and benign Spirit never rests upon his heart, hardened and seared by the dominant law of selfishness; and hence, O misery supreme, no gushing forth of generous feeling, love, and kindness, is ever witnessed there, to fertilise and bless. The heart, to be happy, must be an all-embracing heart, like the heart of God, and must hold all things for the good of others. The devil holds all things for himself, and this is his misery,

21

a misery from which he cannot escape, for it is himself. And hence, though as the god of this world he has much, yet in reality he has nothing, for he cannot get away from himself to enjoy it. All his vast powers centre in himself; like so many chains, they bind him to the central fire of selfishness which consumes him: he never has turned, he never can, he never will of himself turn his face towards that blessed Sun of LOVE whose beams could thaw his awful nature into fruitfulness and joy, and scatter for ever the dreadful winter of hate, covetousness, and despair, which for ever feed upon his mighty heart, and create an eternal desolation in that spirit which once stood erect and brightest before the throne of God. Now, by covetousness men are, as we have observed, assimilated to Satan and fitted for his society; and to the place for which men fit themselves by their sins, God's Word declares they shall go. And, reader, canst thou conceive of anything more awful than this? Picture to thyself a number of covetous men compelled to live together in the same house with no other society for one hundred years— what a scene of moral ruin and misery thou wouldst witness! Canst thou not imagine, that, as these men became less and less human under the influence of their darling sin, how they would torment each other, and even delight themselves in their mutually inflicted pains? Think, then, reader, of hell, with its covetous prince and his children—their state, the ages they have been and must be together; and thy thought, if serious, will give a terrible,—and it is right that it should,—a terrible emphasis to these solemn words of the Great Teacher, "Take heed, and beware of covetousness."

But it is possible some may inquire how they are to escape this all-besetting sin. Can the dreadful chains by which it binds the spirit to the regions of woe be broken? They can: the hands of that God-man who spoiled Satan, and which were nailed to the tree for our sins, can break them. Dost thou ask how? by leading thee to believe in Himself, and to look constantly to Him for strength to overcome this sin as every other. Dost thou doubt this? see it exemplified in the publican of old (Luke xix. 8). Faith will enable thee to bring thy heart near to the heart of Christ, and here it will lose its covetousness, and thou wilt realise for thyself the great truth uttered by the Apostle, "For none of us liveth to himself, and no man dieth to himself; for whether we live, we live unto the Lord; or whether we die, we die unto the Lord: whether we live, therefore, or die, we are the Lord's." A faith, therefore, that works by love will save the soul even from the deadly embraces of covetousness; but it must be a faith that *works* by love. "The liberal man deviseth liberal things, and by liberal things he shall stand." This order must not be inverted; many imagine they are to stand by covetousness, and to fall by liberality,. But, no; God declares we are to *stand* by liberality. Let our faith prayerfully embrace this fact, and practise it, and covetousness shall not claim us as its slaves.

" In vain do wealthy mortals toil,
   And heap their shining dust in vain,
Look down and scorn the humble poor,
   And boast their lofty hills of gain.

Their golden cordials cannot ease
   Their pained hearts or aching heads,
Nor fright nor bribe approaching death
   From glittering roofs and downy beds.

The lingering, the unwilling soul
· The dismal summons must obey,
And bid a long, a sad farewell
   To the pale lump of lifeless clay.

Thence they are huddled to the grave,
   Where kings and slaves have equal thrones;
Their bones without distinction lie
   Amongst the heap of meaner bones."

WATTS.

                        •   Christ is the only
Mass that e'er can save the soul! His precious
And atoning blood, once spilt, for ever cleansed
And purified the church. He is alone,
The Altar, Sacrifice, and Priest: yea, ALL
A sinner needs to cleanse and save.

"Two things may quiet any man's conscience under the
greatest guilt. 1 Is there not a sufficient sacrifice? Is there
·not satisfaction and atonement in the blood of Christ? Is not
this a sufficient sacrifice? 2. Is it thine? This I know unbelief is apt to stagger at; but do but lay the hand of thy faith
upon the head of the sacrifice, and confess and forsake thy sins,
and all that Christ hath done shall be as effectual for thy good
as if thou thyself hadst suffered, yea, infinitely more."—S.
MATHER.

"Here is mercy in its yearning tenderness; grace in its
boundless liberality; power in its mightiest operations; wisdom
in its sweetest deepest contrivances; faithfulness in its stability;
holiness in all its beauty; justice in all its glory; God's whole
will perfectly expressed and responded to; and all these attributes the portion of the sinner, who trusts in the Saviour, all
honoured by his deliverance from hell, and restoration to the
glory of God."—*Our Great High·Priest.*
                                        REV. J. COX.

The One Offering;

OR,

THE CHRISTIAN'S REST.

" For by one offering he hath perfected for ever them that are sanctified."—Heb. x. 12.

THERE is something very delightful in the contemplation of perfection—a finished thing is generally loved. For this reason the smallest expression of Divine power has more charms for us than the most choice productions of man. We look upon a little flower made by God, as it hides its head in the grass, with more pleasure in this particular than the most classic book, ornate temple, or ingenious instrument. And we love in thought to ascend far above all worlds to the contemplation of the Great Eternal, and far away from all sin and imperfection to lay ourselves down at His feet, to muse over the absolutely perfect, in the hope that, at some future period, through the mediation of Christ, we shall lose all our imperfections in the beams of His ineffable glory.

Now we have to contemplate a perfect work —the one offering of Jesus, with the result of that perfection—" He hath by His one offering for ever perfected the sanctified." We pity the man who does not understand this language; whatever he may know of other things, being ignorant of this, his learning will be of little service to him. We are surrounded with the expressions of the physical power of God, minute and diversified, and perfection is written upon them all; but here we have a medium through which His moral attributes display themselves in all their unsullied majesty and glory. The sun, and the moon, and the stars are but so many shining letters in the name of God; but could we put them all together, pile them up in one vast pyramid, blazing and burning with a light above the brightness of the sun, still it would not spell out to us so much of God's character as may be seen written upon the one offering of Christ. God by one act brought this vast world into existence *by* Him who offered Himself up upon its surface, and by a series of touches chastened and subdued, beautified and ultimately subordinated it to *man;* and as we gaze upon this finished temple, and think of the one act which bade it spring forth out of nothing, and the repeated strokes which fluted its columns, carpeted the floor, and painted the ceiling, we wonder and adore. But when we contemplate the one offering of Christ, what it embodies and what it has accomplished, our wonder and adoration is enhanced a thousandfold. That which the many offerings of the law could not accomplish, Jesus accomplishes by *one*. The creature offered up by the creature could not reach the ultimate design of God, but *Himself* presented through the creature, accomplished at once and for ever the work. This last act of Jesus was but the climax of a series by which the spirituality of the law was brought out and satisfied, for Christ worked out the spirituality of the law as well by deeds as by words, and the perfection of the church ensured. To reach this grand consummation, to which all the types and sacrifices of the law pointed, Jesus became incarnate—God and the creature became *one*. The glory which the heaven of heavens could not contain is for a time veiled in a temple of clay. "Out of Zion, the perfection of beauty, God hath shined." From the womb of a virgin comes forth a child whom the angels worship, while the earth recognises the footprints of its adorable Creator. Well might the angelic throng touch their harps afresh, and the shepherds of Bethlehem join in their song, when the Son of God stepped from His throne into a manger, and the Ancient of days appeared in an infant of time. From the moment of His birth does His work commence, fully conformed to the law from the breasts of His mother to the grave. He assumed the nature that had sinned, though not a sinful nature, that He might reach its sin, and for ever put it away. This He accomplished by bearing its penalty. Say some, he could not have endured the precise penalty due to sin, for eternity enters into the sufferings of the lost. True; but does eternity enter into the essence of punishment, or belong rather to the inability of the creature, who is not strong enough to bear the whole *at once?* Say some, the humanity of Christ suffered only, and, therefore, it was impossible that could have borne *all* the curse, suffering, and misery due to the myriads redeemed. Who shall say what humanity *could* bear as sustained by the Divine?· Upheld by Almighty power, we believe it *did* bear a tornado of wrath which must have sought to expend itself upon a guilty church, for ever, but in vain. "You talk mysteries;" yes, sacred to a believing heart. The precise penalty—impossible! what! wrath, anger, remorse, despair? Do these belong to the essence of punishment, or arise out of the sinner's consciousness that he never can meet the requisitions of justice? If Christ did not bear the precise penalty threatened, what relation have His sufferings to the law? If He bore but part, then to that extent must judgment go by default. In the theory of perfect equivalent, men may find difficulties; but does not its denial involve greater? We find it easier to believe even *it* than those which, while they aim to destroy it, put nothing implicitly and fairly in its place, but leave us to search in vain for what it is in the one " one offering" of Christ, of such ineffable, such unutterable value, that those who are embraced by it are eternally perfected. Penitent sinner, dost thou ask what it is? It is the SATISFACTION which Christ gave, *really* gave, to the justice of God for thy sins. That justice simply demanded that which was *right*. Christ yielded that, neither more nor less;—standing in thy room and place, a surety for thee, by the purpose of God made *one* with thee, He bore all the wrath, curse and suffering due to thy sins, that thou mightest escape. Thou canst never understand what it cost Him,—what He suffered. The depths of those waters of sorrow in which he was baptized will never be fathomed by thee, and when thou dost approach them let it be with holy awe; put off thy shoes from off thy feet, for the place whereon thou standest is holy ground. Let not Speculation place her cold hand upon thy heart, and avoid the mere metaphysician when thou dost approach the cross of Christ. The eye of the former may be keen, but you look in vain for a tear ; while the latter, counting the stripes of Jesus, says, they fell upon a creature's back, and that so many and no more could be endured before death seized his victim. They take the *fact* you see that Jesus

died. "Shake hands," say they, "over this."
"Oh, no," says Faith, "'tis its *significance* that
constitutes its worth, that saves my soul, that
sanctifies my heart, and lifts me upwards towards
the throne of God; superficial views of the justice
of God lead to superficial views of the sufferings
of Christ, and superficial views of the sufferings
of Christ lead to similar views of the nature of
sin." "I see no mystery in the cross of Christ,"
says Reason, and, putting her fingers into His
bleeding wounds, she says they are not deep.
Says Faith, "They are deep enough to hide all
the sins of the Church, for He has by His one
offering for ever perfected them that are sanctified,
and—

> "'Here I'll sit for ever viewing
>   Mercy's streams in streams of blood;
> Precious drops my soul bedewing,
>   Plead and claim my peace with God.'"

For ever perfected the sanctified? perfected,
how? By the removal of sin, the procuring of
pardon, justification, sanctification. In relation
to what? The law of God, the lawgiver—God
Himself, if you please; the act of justification
which passed upon the Head, when He arose
from the dead, embraced the members. In the
blood of Jesus the church lost at once and for
ever all her guilt. The huge burden of all her
sins He left in His sepulchre, never to be seen
again; and now in the eyes of absolute purity she

stands without a spot. The law with its ten eyes
looks at her both within and without, and declares
her faultless. Holiness smiles upon her, and placing
her arms around her, lifts her to the very bosom
of God. Amid the streaming effulgence of heaven
her robes are white, and in beauty and brightness
outvie the clothing of cherubim and seraphim
before the throne. Here we have a perfection
not built upon the creature's excellence or work,
but the perfections and toil of the Son of God.
Here we behold the soul again restored to its
rightful Lord, and more than paradise regained.
We see it clothed in a beauty more glorious than
even that which sin took away, and imperishable
as the life of God,—a perfection built upon the
finished work of Christ and secured and embraced
by all the attributes of Deity, and destined to display itself in the undying bliss of myriads through
the countless ages of eternity. O glorious bridegroom! O transcendent bride! O wondrous
sacrifice, which thus consummates a union pregnant with such divine results! O my soul, amid
the many things which the passing pageant of
this world constantly presents to thy view, and
by which it would distract thy attention from
heavenly things, let the one offering of Jesus
never be overlooked. Let this be the central
object of all thy meditations, as it is the procuring
cause of all thy bliss. See thou but one offering
in the book of God and amid all the varied offer-

ings of the law; see this world reared but as an
altar for its presentation to God. Behold it as the
central point of time, the pivot of providence, and
destined to exert an infallible and holy influence
over the present and eternal destiny of myriads
yet unborn. To this great offering come, and on
it present thy offerings, that they may be per-
fumed and accepted by the great I AM. Art
thou anxious to know if the one offering of Jesus
embraces thee? He has by His *one* offering perfected them that are sanctified. Those who were
set apart by the Father's love, chosen in Jesus,
for whom He stood surety—whom He received
as a precious gift from His Father's hand—ah!
but who are they, say you? Those who believe
in and love Jesus; those who obey and follow
Jesus; those who hunger and thirst after Jesus;
who not only desire to be saved by Jesus, but to
be conformed to Him—these are the sanctified.
But while seeking to be sanctified, believer, look
not to *it*, but to Jesus; look not at the perfection
thou hast reached as the basis of thy hope, or it
will be hidden from thy eyes; but look to the
perfection of Jesus,—to His one offering. Here,
while labouring to glorify thy God, thou wilt find
a perfection which will never fail thee, but, in the
midst of all thy conscious sins and infirmities,
will ever remain the same, and will support thy
hope amid all the billows of temptation, the trials
of life, and the dark waves of death.

"Jesus, thy blood and righteousness,
My beauty is, my glorious dress;
'Midst flaming worlds, in these arrayed,
With joy shall I lift up my head."

From these observations, the reader, it is hoped, will perceive that there is an indissoluble connexion between the finished work of Christ, and the ultimate salvation of all who are embraced by it. If the Atonement, therefore, of Christ embraces all men, then all men are perfected by it, and who can perish? Ah! but faith is needed. True, but faith creates nothing, but simply apprehends what is. From this stand-point, too, of eternal truth, we see the sin of the Catholic priest, who declares that he constantly offers up the Son of God afresh in the unbloody sacrifice of the Mass, and, by thus *acting*, as constantly impeaches and denies the perfection of the sacrifice of Christ. Upon this huge, monstrous, Christ-denying lie the entire system of Rome is built; take this away, and the vast, voluptuous temple of superstition falls. Let us aim to take it away, not by using her weapons, by emulating her spirit, or by thundering forth anathemas, but by making known the truth. The death of Christ which is her weakness, is our strength; by her many offerings she shall die, by the one offering of Christ we shall live. This is the knife by which only we can kill the pride and enmity of man; the lever in the hand of faith by which all false systems shall ultimately be overturned. Upon the one offering of Jesus, as the most grand and sublime *reality* which God Himself ever presented to the faith and affections of an intelligent being, may we, therefore, in simple and childlike faith, live, and, thus fed and sustained, may we labour; and having accomplished all the work assigned us through the same blessed medium, may we enter into that rest the enjoyment of which it has procured and en-sured to the perfected just!

" Rest, weary soul!
The penalty is borne, the ransom paid,
For all thy sins full satisfaction made;
Strive not thyself to do what Christ has done;
Take the free gift, and make the joy thine own.
No more by pangs of guilt and fear distrest—
   Rest, sweetly rest!

   Rest, weary heart!
From all thy silent griefs, and secret pain,
Thy profitless regrets, and longings vain;
Wisdom and love have ordered all the past,
All shall be blessedness and light at last;
Cast off the cares that have so long opprest—
   Rest, sweetly rest!

   Rest, weary head!
Lie down to slumber in the peaceful tomb,
Light from above has broken through its gloom,
Here, in the place where once thy Saviour lay,
Where He shall wake thee on a future day,
Like a tired child upon its mother's breast—
   Rest, sweetly rest!

Rest, spirit free!
In the green pastures of the heavenly shore,
Where sin and sorrow can approach no more ;
With all the flock by the Good Shepherd fed,
Beside the streams of life eternal led,
Forever with thy God and Saviour blest—
    Rest, sweetly rest!"

H. L. L. in *Family Paper*.

"Hast thou a care, whose pressure dread
Expels sweet slumber from thy bed?
To thy Redeemer take that care,
And change anxiety to prayer."

MRS. A. JULIUS.

"The green apple does not like to be twisted and torn from the tree; but the ripened fruit that has no more need for the root's sap, drops easily off. Trust in the Lord, when a soul attains it, loosens every other bond, and makes it easy to let go all which the world gives. When you feel your footing firm in the peace of God, you will not be afraid though the earth should sink away from beneath you."—"*Illustrations of the Book of Proverbs,*" by REV. W. ARNOT.

"It is easy to persuade Papists to lean on priests and saints, on old rags and painted pictures—on any idol; but it is hard to get a Protestant to trust in the living God."—*Ibid.*

"Popery sails with the stream when it bids men trust, for this falls in with a tendency of nature; but it puts forward to receive the confiding soul a dead idol, whose presence is no rebuke to indulged sin."—*Ibid.*

The Believer's Great Lesson;

OR,

THE CONDITION OF PEACE.

*" Thou wilt keep him in perfect peace, whose mind is stayed
on thee : because he trusteth in thee."*—Isaiah xxvi. 3.

THERE are many very beautiful, congruous, and
harmonious things to be found in this lower creation : but none more beautiful, congruous, and
harmonious than that of a mind " stayed upon
God." But how rare a thing is this ; and how
seldom do we meet with it. There are myriads
of minds to be found in the world, but of how
few comparatively can it be affirmed that they
are stayed upon God.

Man is, indeed, a wanderer at a distance from
his home ; and his mind roams through the universe like an orphan seeking rest, and finding
none. Upon the flower of worldly pleasure his
mind frequently settles, like a bee seeking to ex-
tract from it the honey of contentment, but in

vain. Wealth, learning, fame, successively present themselves before him; and enamoured with their charms, he seeks to find rest in their embrace, and as constantly fails. Any object, indeed, he will for a time eulogise and receive, rather than the God who made him; and against the requisitions of whose mercy he constantly fights. In the world of mind, therefore, a mind stayed upon God is a rare thing; and it may be profitable to notice some of its characteristics, and the peace which stands connected with its privilege. Such a mind is—

1. *A regenerate mind.*—Sin has made man degenerate; alive to anything and everything rather than God. Under its influence the mind gravitates *from* God, and that perpetually, from the cradle to the grave. At regeneration, a principle of spiritual life is infused into the soul by the Holy Spirit, under the influence of which it again turns to God, as its Great Parent, to find refuge and peace. No human power can accomplish this; it is the work of God. "No man can come unto me," said Christ, "except the Father which hath sent me draw him."

2. *Instructed.*—A mind stayed upon God does not rest upon Him like a stone in the ocean, without intelligence or feeling; but is possessed of both. Such a mind will be found to be instructed, and that by God himself. "All thy children shall be taught of the Lord, and great shall be the

peace of thy children." The character of God is known—for " this is life eternal to know thee, the only true God, and Jesus Christ whom thou hast sent." " God, who commanded the light to shine out of darkness, hath shined into our hearts, to give the light of the knowledge of the glory of God in the face of Jesus Christ." God out of Christ, by reason of his Holiness, is a consuming fire ; but in Christ, all his perfections are so har-monised, as to become the couch of the soul. Christ is the mirror in which God is seen by the believer ; and here he learns how He can pardon his sins ; how He can be just, and yet the justifier of the ungodly ; and under the influence of these perceptions he comes, and with child-like confi-dence drops upon the bosom of paternal love. The rest, therefore, of the soul, when it is of God, is a sublimely intelligent rest ; the mind is at home amid the perfections of Deity ; is hushed to rest by the very attributes of Jehovah, and be-comes a medium by which they are perpetually reflected. God looks upon the mind thus blessed with holy delight and complacency, and says, " This is my rest, here will I dwell, for I have desired it ;" while the soul responds, " Whom have I in heaven but Thee, and there is none upon the earth that I desire beside Thee. My heart and flesh fail, but God is the strength of my heart and my portion for ever."

3. *Believing mind.*—" Thou wilt keep him in

perfect peace, whose mind is stayed on thee:
because he *trusteth in thee.*" It is by believing we
enter into rest. It is by faith that the hand of
God raises the soul to himself. "THOU wilt keep
him in peace." The waters of the human mind
God calms by the oil of faith; faith is a balm, a
sedative for all its woes; but the hand of God's
Spirit must apply it. Faith is an anchor to the
soul, sure and steadfast, and which entereth into
that within the veil; but God fixes that anchor
upon the rock of Christ, and thus fulfils the promise, " *Thou* wilt keep Him in perfect peace,
whose mind is stayed on thee: because he trusteth
in thee."

4. *Weaned mind.*—" My soul is like a weaned
child," said the psalmist. His soul had but one
Master—God. The carnal mind has many lords,
who make sad havoc of its powers, and who help
themselves to its strength and peace as they please
—hence its distractions and sorrows. The soul,
therefore, can never be *itself* until it comes to God.
Until the King takes possession of His throne, all
the subjects will rebel. To bring a man, therefore, to God, is to bring him *to himself.* A mind
stayed upon God is weaned from all created
things, and being weaned from them gains power
over them, and can subordinate them to their
legitimate uses. When the mind is content to be
nothing, that God may be all and in all, perfect
peace and prevalent victory is the result; and

those thus blessed even now *reign* with Christ, and are made "kings and priests unto God."

5. *Sanctified.*—If the mind, like a vessel, becomes emptied of itself and filled with Christ, we are sure who has accomplished the work. The GREAT SANCTIFIER only can purify the affections, and lead the mind to desire and realize its true rest in God. And how loving, yet invincible, is His work. It is His kind hand removes all our vain refuges until the heart of Jesus becomes the home of the spirit. When contemplating man's wrecked, forlorn, and storm-tossed spirit, at rest upon the bosom of its God, let us never forget that this shining gem in this universe of darkness and uncertainty, is especially and emphatically the work of God's Spirit.

But we have to notice the result of the mind being stayed upon God—"*perfect peace.*"

This peace is a peace of harmony; the soul is in harmony with God, itself, and the world.

1. *In harmony with God.*—This is essential to real peace. That which is true of our physical constitution, is no less true of our moral. The body is an exquisitely-adjusted machine, every part of which must work in accordance with the intention of the Great Mechanician who put it together, or health, which is indeed the peace of the body, will be absent. And so with the soul; the intelligence which dwells in the midst of the complicated bodily mechanism, with all its facul-

ties, must be in accordance with God's moral laws in order to peace. When the mind is stayed upon Christ, this is accomplished, and peace is the result.

2. *In harmony with itself.*—This follows as the result of the former. A mind in harmony with God will be in harmony with itself, even as the planets of the solar system being in harmony with the sun, are in harmony with themselves: the effect of this harmony is peace.

3. *In harmony with the universe.*—A mind stayed upon God is a meek mind; and the meek shall inherit the earth. Such a mind will wisely use the world, and not abuse it; will be able frequently to say, under the influence of holy and sublime enjoyment,

"Creation's heir, the world, the world is mine."

Even the seeming discord of the world will become music to the soul in harmony with God. The mind, attuned to its highest and sublimest function, like an Æolian harp touched by the fingers of nature, will give forth its most latent music, and yield in undying strains the richest melodies of heaven—the key-note of each and all, however, being peace: "And the work of righteousness shall be peace; and the effect of righteousness, quietness and assurance for ever."

This peace, however, is spoken of as a "perfect peace:"—

1. Because it is complete in itself, and contains the germ of present and everlasting bliss.

2. Because it is the fruit of God's most perfect Spirit, harmonising the powers of the soul, and bringing them into accordance with God, and truth, and happiness.

3. On account of the element of perpetuity it contains, this perfect peace never fails the soul. It is not affected by the changes of time; it may be compared to a river issuing from the throne of God and the Lamb, and flowing on without let or hindrance through the waste places of time to the deep and quiet ocean of eternity.

4. It perfects the character; it frees the mind from the reign of slavish fear, doubt, and uncertainty, and fits for heaven.

We have said, that a mind stayed upon God is a beautiful thing; it is like a child in peace upon its mother's breast; like a beautiful mirror reflecting the glory of God; a well-tuned instrument ever discoursing His praise. Oh that through the teaching of God's Spirit this privilege may become unceasingly ours!

· From these reflections, we may learn how foolish it is to seek for happiness apart from the favour of God, seeing that the conditions of happiness depend upon the soul's being brought into harmony with God. And what an encouraging consideration, to the most disordered and degraded, that God in Christ speaks to us, and

23

exhorts us to look to Him, that we may be saved. The soul is, indeed, like a broken harp; but God can repair it; and this He accomplishes, not by education, philosophy, or morality, but by bringing it to Himself, by the power of a living faith in a crucified Saviour, the merits of His Son, and the renewing of His Spirit. Thus is it, dear reader, that the hand of Divine Mercy reaches the soul in the midst of its most dreadful struggles with sin and death, to raise it from its dangers and sorrows to the very heights of glory and renown. "TRUST YE (THEREFORE) IN THE LORD FOR EVER; for in the Lord JEHOVAH IS EVERLASTING STRENGTH."

"Thou hidden Love of God, whose height,
    Whose depth unfathom'd no man knows,
I see from far thy beauteous light,
    Inly I sigh for thy repose.
        My heart is pain'd, nor can it be
        At rest, till it finds rest in Thee.

Thy secret voice invites me still
    The sweetness of Thy yoke to prove;
And fain I would; but though my will
    Seems fix'd, yet wide my passions rove,
        And hindrances obstruct the way;
        I aim at Thee, but from Thee stray.

'Tis mercy all, that Thou hast brought
    My mind to seek her peace in Thee;
Yet, while I seek, but find Thee not,
    No peace my wandering soul shall see.
        Oh, when shall all my wanderings end,
        And all my steps to heaven tend!

Is there a thing beneath the sun
  That strives with Thee my heart to share?
Ah, tear it thence and reign alone,
  The Lord of every motion there.
    Then shall my heart from earth be free
    When it hath found repose in Thee.

Each moment draw from earth away
  My heart, that lowly waits Thy call.
Speak to my inmost soul and say,
  'I am thy Love, thy God, thy All.'
    To feel Thy power, to hear Thy voice,
    To taste Thy love, be all my choice!"

" A seeming truth, and yet beware
The half truth only may be there.
The man is not of soul alone,
But soul and body knit in one;
And will the Maker look for less
Than the *whole* being's earnestness?"

WM. SAWYER, ESQ.,
· "*Lays of the Sanctuary.*"

"The turning which constitutes salvation is, supremely, all God's gift, and subordinately, all the doing of man. From the spring-head in the heart, to the outermost streams of life, He makes all things new; and yet the man himself must, at God's bidding, turn from all iniquity."

REV. W. ARNOT,
"*Illustrations of the Book of Proverbs.*"

𝔄𝔭𝔬𝔰𝔱𝔬𝔩𝔦𝔠 𝔓𝔯𝔢𝔞𝔠𝔥𝔦𝔫𝔤;

OR,

THE MANIFESTATION OF TRUTH TO THE CONSCIENCE.

" By manifestation of the truth commending ourselves to every man's conscience in the sight of God."—2 Cor. iv. 2.

WHAT God as a moral Governor claims from men in general who hear the Gospel of His Son, and *how* those claims are to be set forth by those to whom is entrusted the proclamation of the tidings of mercy, have been and must continue to be, points of intense interest and prayerful anxiety to the earnest Christian. When we reflect that a mistake in reference to the former, will not only dishonour God, but may be the means of misleading men to their eternal ruin, how solemnly important it is, that we should seek wisdom at the fountain-head; that so men may neither be deceived by our words, nor alienated by our manner, but that, emulating the conduct of the Apostle, "by the

23*

manifestation of the truth we may commend ourselves to every man's conscience in the sight of
God." The contemplation of these words may
tend to the elucidation of the points to which
reference is made above, and we will notice three
things :—conscience, work, and manner.

Conscience.—Much has been written respecting
this by many, and to but little purpose. Some
have made use of their reason to destroy con-
sciecne, thinking that by so doing they should get
rid of their responsibility. These men may be
viewed as moral suicides, both in reference to
themselves and society. They have argued thus:
—Many are to be found among the heathen who
have not and never had a conscience, and, therefore, it is evident that God makes some men
without a conscience, and if without a conscience,
without responsibility. But does the absence of
a thing prove the normal condition of the thing
from which it is absent? Men may be found
without natural health, but does this prove that
God made or meant them to be so? And ought
we not to distinguish between the existence of a
thing and the evidences of its existence? The
eye is a beautiful optical instrument, perfect in
itself; and though it should present no object to
the mind in the midst of darkness, still the person
favoured with its possession would not be justified
in coming to the conclusion, that because he could
not see under such circumstance such an organ did

not exist. So man may have the faculty by which to distinguish right from wrong, though the darkness of ignorance may for a time prevent its exercise. But let light from heaven stream inward upon it through the truth, and we soon shall find that the monitor is there, though for a long time lulled to sleep by his own sin or the sins of his parents. Here is a train of gunpowder, but we cannot see it, and have no evidence of its existence; but let a spark though ever so small reach it, and what a sudden explosion! And here is a conscience altogether dead, and affording no evidences of its existence, but the omnipotent Spirit lets fall a spark of truth upon it, and what a terrible storm in the soul!—the man is killed in his apprehensions, while all his false hopes are blown to pieces around him. It was so with the Apostle Paul. He was once alive, he tells us, without the law. It appeared as though he had no conscience in relation to it—but when the law *came*, brought by the agency of the Holy Spirit, when its true character was opened up to his mind, his spiritual perception of the extent of its requirements pierced his slumbering conscience like a knife, and it arose and pronounced the verdict of condemnation upon him, and he stood a dead man in the eye of law, with his false hope slain by his side. We cannot, therefore, argue from what a man is in a diseased condition, to what he is when in health, either naturally or spiritually.

Nor does it follow, because conscience does not trouble a man, that, therefore, he has none; for in a moment, by the agency of truth, His Almighty Spirit can demonstrate the contrary in the experience of any man, however ignorant or depraved he may be. We think that if it be granted to us that man has a soul as well as a body, we could, arguing from analogy, prove that man must have a conscience. Take a needle and pierce any part of the body; what is the result?—pain; and what is that but God's sentinel upon the walls of our frail habitation, placed there by Him in love, to warn us when we are violating any of the laws of our physical being, that we may not destroy ourselves? And can we for a moment suppose that God would thus care for the material and perishable, without a corresponding care for the safety of the immaterial and imperishable? We believe that what we term conscience in the soul of man, *is* this expression of God's superlative love of that immortal inmate, and intended by Him to preserve us from the violation of the laws of our moral being, even as pain is by Him intended to be subservient to the same result in reference to the body. Though nations therefore may be found, whose conscience has been partially or wholly destroyed by their ancestors, and individuals who have, by their own sins, consigned to death the friend whose faithful warnings and reproofs it was their duty, and would most assuredly have been their happiness to have preserved, still of men in general, even the most ignorant and depraved, we may safely affirm that there is in them a moral sense, a mind capable of discrimination between right and wrong, termed conscience, and which gives them a relation of responsibility to the law and moral government of God. This conscience, however, may and does exist in men in various states; it may be found in a state of death, Eph. ii. 1; anxiety, Acts ii. 37; peace, Rom. v. 1.

Now the Apostles—while with all plainness of speech they endeavoured to make known the truth of the Gospel to the mind, and by their appeals to the facts of human consciousness or experience, as agreeing with the declarations of the Word of God, sought to gain for their message a believing reception as coming from God—never lost sight of the various *states* of conscience to which we have referred, but sought through the medium of certain adapted truths found in the Word of God, to reach them, and to produce certain specific results in relation to each. It may be instructive for us to notice these results, and how they sought to produce them. Their object in reference to the dead conscience would be to wound, alarm, and arouse it; in other words, in dependence upon the Holy Spirit to vitalise it. This they endeavoured to compass by :—

1. Opening up the nature and spirituality of

God's law, and the truth in general, to the understanding, and by reasoning and persuasion; as
may be seen most fully exemplified in the Epistle
of Paul to the Galatians, and the course he pursued with his unbelieving brethren at Antioch.
Acts xiii. 14.

2. By charging home certain sins upon the consciences of those who were known to have com-
mitted them. Acts ii. 23.

3. By warnings: we shall cite but one, uttered
by Paul and Barnabas to the unbelieving Jews.
Acts xiii. 46. "Then Paul and Bárnabas waxed
bold, and said, It was necessary that the Word of
God should first have been spoken to you: but
seeing ye put it from you, and judge yourselves
unworthy of everlasting life, lo, we turn to the
Gentiles." These words are very striking, and
plainly declare that the Apostles did not permit
men to go from beneath the sound of their voice
under the impression that their unbelief and destitution of salvation were to be traced to the sovereignty of God, but to their own ignorance and
enmity; they traced it to their *own act and deed,*
and threw the blame of their own condemnation
upon themselves—"*seeing ye judge yourselves* unworthy of everlasting life." The heavy chain of
personal responsibility men are perpetually endea-
vouring, by all kinds of sophistries and the teaching of Satan, to loosen from themselves and to
fasten upon God, vainly striving to throw the

blame of their eternal ruin upon him, the Apostles constantly sought, by their teaching, and the
manifestation of the truth, to fasten again upon
them, with the design and prayer that they, feeling its pressure, might be brought to seek for
mercy; or if they did not, that the righteousness
of God might the more abundantly appear in
their condemnation. "We are unto God," said
he, "a sweet savour of Christ, in them that are
saved, and in them that perish."

4. By exhortation. Thus the Apostle upon
Mars-hill—"and the times of this ignorance God
winked at; but now commandeth all men everywhere to repent." And the motive he brings
before them to incite them to repentance in dependence upon God's Spirit was not derived from
any national good to be procured by it, or temporal favour, but from the day of judgment and
their eternal destiny in relation to it.

The same course also was pursued by the Apostle Peter, who did not hesitate to call upon Simon,
the sorcerer, to repent of his sin, and to pray to
God that it might be forgiven him. "Repent
therefore," said he, "of this thy wickedness, and
pray God, if perhaps the thought of thy heart
may be forgiven thee. For *I perceive that thou art
in the gall of bitterness, and in the bond of iniquity.*"
Here we have a man exhorted to repentance and
prayer, that his sin may be forgiven him; and,
of course, faith in the merits of Christ must have

been involved, for there can be no pardon without faith in the atoning sacrifice of Jesus. And the reason why the Apostle so exhorted him was, that he perceived him to be unconverted—"I perceive," said he, "thou art in the gall of bitterness," &c.— the very reason why some would not have so exhorted him, but have thought it extremely wrong and a great folly to do so.

Our Saviour also exhorted sinners to seek their salvation—"While ye have light believe in the light, that ye may be the children of light." These words were addressed to the people indiscriminately. It has been admitted that the appellation "children of light," is never applied to any but real Christians; it follows, therefore, that .Christ exhorted men in general to seek their salvation, and to follow after real religion. Some have affirmed that by these words our Saviour simply exhorts to natural faith, and that those who so believed and received him as the Messiah, might be compared to children of light when contrasted with those who rejected Him, although not saved by their faith, or really converted in heart to God. But it has been admitted that the phraseology is never used but in reference to those who are really converted to God; and to admit that Christ exhorted to the exercise of such natural faith, as the extent of man's obligation, would be equal to an affirmation that He was broken in the aim of His ministry—that on some occasions He exhorted to that which on other occasions he condemned. This is apparent from the parable of the "wise and foolish virgins," in which He condemns those who were satisfied with a mere form of religion, and terms them *foolish* for taking a lamp without oil. But if He exhorted them not to seek grace, but merely to a faith which left them with their hearts alienated and really in the world notwithstanding their profession, a faith which left them natural men still, and as such at enmity with God, how could he justly term them foolish virgins? Could not such at the day of judgment reply to Christ and say, Why term us foolish for being what you simply exhorted us to be? You did not really call upon us to seek grace or the salvation of our souls; and have we not heard your own servants, upon the ground of your own revealed will, ridicule duty-faith, and affirm that it was folly to exhort us to seek the one thing needful? But can the reader believe that the exhortations of Christ for the most part were intended to direct self-righteous men to a *dead morality*, which He condemned, to believe with the faith of devils —to repent, while at the same time they hate, and at last die in their sins and perish for ever? Yet all these things follow if Christ exhorted men to a faith which left them *natural* men; for a natural man is a carnal man, and the carnal mind is enmity against God; it is not subject to the law of God, neither indeed can it be. If it be asserted that

24

Christ did call upon men to exercise such a faith,
and has made it incumbent upon His ministers to
do so now, we should be inclined to ask upon
what ground and to what law such a faith stands
related? We certainly think it passing strange
that, standing in the midst of a self-righteous
people, He should exhort them to a faith which
was *dead*, not having a spiritual root, and that
He of whom it was said most emphatically that
He came to save the *lost*, should direct almost all
His efforts to the production of a grace which left
men still in their sins, and exposed to eternal
wrath. If this is not German neology, it is certainly something worse than negative theology,
as we have no doubt the day of eternity will
declare.

We could cite almost any number of passages
to prove our position—that the Apostles sought
to arouse the dead consciences of men by exhorting them to seek the salvation of their souls—but
shall content ourselves with but two. Our Saviour,
addressing the Pharisees, said—"Labour not for
the meat which perisheth, but for that meat which
endureth unto everlasting life, which the Son of
man shall give unto you; for Him hath God the
Father sealed." Then said they unto Him, "*What
shall we do*, that we might work the works of
God?" Jesus answered and said unto them,
"This is the work of God, that ye believe on
Him whom He hath sent." The people here, as

elsewhere, were all for *working.* "What shall we do?" said they. "This is your duty," said Christ, "not to work at all, but simply *to believe.*" This is what God demands of you, that you "believe on Him whom He hath sent." And the motive to this was not that their nation might be spared the judgments of God, or that they might have a less degree of torment in hell, but that they might have EVERLASTING LIFE. To a curious speculative character, and there are many such, who put a question to our Lord as to whether few would be saved, He said, "Strive to enter in at the straight gate." Upon this we cannot now enlarge, but we would simply add, that we think our Saviour dealt wisely with this man, who was but a type of too many in our day; our supreme concern should be to know that we are interested in Christ; with the number to be saved, whether few or many, we have nothing to do.

To what we have here stated many objections, we have no doubt, will be brought. Some will say, Why exhort the sinner to seek when he is dead? To which we reply, that the rule of a man's obligation is not his ability or inability, but the commands of God, which commands are built upon His eternal law, which law makes it incumbent upon man that, in whatever form the will of God is made known to him, he should receive it, and conform himself to it. And if it be absurd to exhort men to believe because they cannot, then it must be equally absurd to open up the law to them, seeing that they have no more power to perceive its spirituality, so as to be savingly convinced of *sin*, than they have to believe the Gospel.

Others may object that to exhort men in general to seek the salvation of their souls is equal to a declaration of insincerity on the part of God, He having determined the salvation of the elect only; to which we reply that these exhortations are not declarative of God's secret intentions, but of the sinner's duty, and intended to show the connexion God has established between the means and the end to be accomplished—viz. faith and the salvation of the soul. God commanded Pharaoh, by the mouth of His servant, to let His people go, but secretly He determined he should not; was God insincere, or was it less Pharoah's duty to have obeyed His command?

But, say some, God has not provided salvation for all. How, then, can all be exhorted to seek? Because obligation to believe does not arise out of provision at all, but out of the eternal law of God. If these explanations are not satisfactory, and do *not* harmonise the doctrine of particular redemption with a free appeal to the sinner's conscience, what then—shall we give up either? God forbid! *Both* being contained in the Word of God, it is of more importance that we should hold and declare both, than that *we* should supply connecting links, to make them harmonise with each other, *as we imagine*. Does God seek this at our hands? Let the reader consider what he must believe if he parts with either, and whether other systems do not present greater difficulties.

Suppose we were to say that the exhortations we have referred to form but the moral instrumentality by which God seeks out His elect, the Spirit of God making them efficient thereto; can this be shown to be inconsistent with the will, wisdom, or Word of God? We should have no objection to let them rest on this ground, especially as God himself has been pleased so to employ them; and this fact one would think might well induce us so to use them.

But we must conclude with a few words on the MANNER or SPIRIT under the influence of which the Apostle sought to accomplish his work —"commending ourselves," he says, "to every man's conscience *in the sight of God.*" It is very evident from this declaration of the Apostle, that, however great the number of persons to whom he addressed himself, he did not lose his Master among them, but kept the eye of his faith steadfastly fixed upon the God whom he served; and among the many important purposes which this would accomplish in his soul, it would certainly lift him above the smile or frown of the creature, and enable him to look at man, simply as man.

24*

Kings or princes might be among his auditors; but what could they be in his estimation compared with the great God in whose presence he stood? The realization also of the Divine presence would also impart fervour and becoming solemnity to his speech. How important is the former; while in reference to the latter what is preaching without it, but a sacred pantomime, a religious make-believe? There is, however, a professional solemnity put on by some, and which is as offensive to God as the levity of the fool; like all unreal things, it is formal, dead, cold, uninteresting, and uninfluential. And there is a solemnity which is sacred, sweet, cheerful, enlivening, elevating, instructive, subduing, and joyous—under the influence of which both the speaker and hearer may smile, sing, and even laugh. We suppose it is so in the temple of heaven, and no less in the spiritual church here, which is but the porch of that temple. This solemnity, however, does not arise out of a man's natural formation, but out of the state of his soul before God, which leads him to be natural because earnest, and the influence of His Holy Spirit, so that it is just one of those things which cannot be counterfeited. The very reality and earnestness of some preachers, together with the sacred joyousness they feel in their Master's work, will sometimes so influence their manner and words as to provoke a smile, which is frequently but expressive of spiritual perception and enjoyment of the truth so advanced; and this shows the folly of those who condemn without discrimination what they imagine to be inconsistent, not with the work of God, but with certain preconceived notions engendered by monotonous ignorance or the canons of respectable formality. Such persons very frequently most require the very things they condemn in a preacher. So completely are they asleep in the grave of formality that the very voice of God himself, as it awakens the dead by their side, is offensive to them, because it arouses them from their slumber, disturbs their sacerdotal vestments, and removes that darling order of things upon which they have stretched themselves for so many years with all the settled complacency and serenity of death. But the holy cheerfulness of the saint, and the smile that lights up his face beneath the beaming forth of God's love through the truth and His Spirit, must not be confounded with the senseless titter of levity. The Apostle never attempted to provoke a smile apart from a moral purpose. He was neither a sanctimonious formalist, nor a religious buffoon. He, at least, could not perceive anything in the great verities he proclaimed—the state of man—the cross of Christ, heaven or hell—to excite laughter in the presence of the great God whom he served; and he forgot not one who had said, "Behold, I am against them that prophesy false dreams, saith the Lord, and do tell them, and cause my people to err by their lies, and by their *lightness;* yet I sent them not, nor commanded them : therefore they shall *not profit* this people at all, saith the Lord."—Jer. xxiii. 32.　May the important truths we have so slightly touched have our most prayerful attention !

> " Lord, preserve us in the faith,
> 　Suffer nought to drive us thence,
> Neither Satan, scorn, nor death;
> 　Be our God and our defence,
> Though the flesh resist Thy will,
> Let Thy word be stronger still.
>
> And when we at last must die,
> 　Oh, assure the sinking heart
> Of the glorious realm on high,
> 　Where thou healest every smart,
> Of the joys unspeakable,
> Where our God would have us dwell."

"A school has risen up at Oxford and elsewhere, in which some of the fundamental doctrines of the Gospel, especially the atonement and the inspiration and authority of the Old Testament, are, if not absolutely denied, yet undermined. The atonement means, as they teach it, nothing more than a manifestation of Divine love, and the putting away of sin by its moral power over the soul, but which has no reference to the authority and majesty of the law and the rectitude of the Divine government; as held by them, it is merely a wonderful instance of fortitude and patience under suffering of the Man of sorrows, and its whole efficacy lies in the influence of those virtues on the human conscience, but not in his death being an expiation of guilt, a vicarious sacrifice of the Son of God. Mercy, according to their view, is the only attribute of the Divine nature displayed in the stupendous transactions of Calvary, while the manifestation of public justice has no provision made for it in their view of the scheme of human redemption. Thus while the name of atonement is retained, and even that reluctantly, the true scriptural idea, as shadowed forth in the sacrifices of the Old Testament and asserted in the pages of the New, is denied and lost. This, I fear, is the error which is insidiously corrupting the theology of some Episcopalians and Nonconformists. From the writers of this class we hear a good deal about 'enlightened and liberal opinions,' 'a rational interpretation of Scriptures,' 'freedom from the prejudices of the schools,' 'extreme views of inspiration,' 'the narrow prejudices which trammel the noble spirit of theology by creeds and catechisms.' And we have been lately told, 'Science is the basis of a rational theology, which is to give the death-blow to superstition.' All this high-sounding praise of modern illumination, pronounced as it is by men whose genius or whose style gives enchantment to their words, is seductive to those young and ardent minds which are exulting in their freedom from the fetters of old systems, and is, I fear, leading some astray from the way of truth."—REV. J. A. JAMES.

Positive Theology;

OR,

THE WHOLE COUNSEL OF GOD.

" Wherefore I take you to record this day that I am pure from the blood of all men. For I have not shunned to declare unto you all the counsel of God."—Acts xx. 26, 27.

WE should never forget that we live in a world which produced a Judas, and that it is the place where Christ was crucified; that the saddest episodes of its history may find a place in our own experience, and that the worst done by the worst may gather a double emphasis from our lives. This world, as of old, has a fair lip but a foul heart; and while professing to love the truth, it behoves us to remember, that, in the person of Christ, it did with truth what it did with virtue—hung it up between two thieves. By pretty words, therefore, we ought not to be deceived; but, if God has opened our hearts, as he did Lydia's of old, to receive His words, we should buckle on our armour

and prepare for the battle.   Men, having departed
from God, are at a distance from the truth.   He
speaks to them, but they do not care to listen to
His voice; or, when they hear, their enmity is too
frequently the only result.   Should our voice,
therefore, be in any degree the echo of the great
Lawgiver's, we may witness a similar result.   From
the language of the Apostle Paul, it is evident that
this was his experience; be affirmed, indeed, in
another place, that the preaching of the Cross was
to the Jews a stumbling-block, and to the Greeks
foolishness; and from his solemn appeal to the
consciences of his hearers, above cited, it is plain
that there are certain truths contained in the
Gospel of Christ to which the minds of men in
general are greatly opposed.   We may very briefly
notice some of those peculiarities of the Gospel
system towards which men ever have and continue
to manifest great enmity.   And there are two
doctrines plainly revealed which generally develop
this latent tendency—Divine sovereignty as it is
manifested and reigns in the salvation of man, and
human responsibility.   Publish the former to the
exclusion of the latter, and men will not find much
fault; on the contrary, it is the direct road to
popularity with numbers; for among the many
bad things sin has introduced into man's heart,
there are all the elements of a Mohammedan fatal-
ism, and he loves to be told that God *so* reigns as
to supersede all his duties and anxieties in refer-

ence to his eternal destiny and that of others; that as a blind man cannot see, so neither can he understand; that as a lame man cannot walk, so neither can he love God. Poor sinner! Ah, this suits the enmity of such poor; this indirect vindication of their *wilful* ignorance and hatred of the light. And, on the other hand, those who fully declare the latter while they repudiate the former, swim bravely with the tide; for men are self-righteous and proud, and care not how responsible they are made, so long as God is not put above them in the matter of their salvation, and they are allowed, in some degree, to share the glory with Him.

The doctrine, too, of divine and *special* influence is exceedingly offensive to many, especially to mere formalists. Such will talk about religion; and, although they think little, and never really pray, are very oracular, and their opinion is quite as good as any one's. "Special influence! Non-sense; we rely upon the Word of Almighty God: no one but ignorant and superstitious people talk so. Special influence! Why, that would involve a change of which we are not conscious; therefore, down with it. Special influence! Why, that would involve the doctrine of special love, and make God a respecter of persons; mere enthusiasm!"

It would be very instructive to trace out how it is that the grand peculiarities of the Gospel—

25

the precious, purifying, exalting, and ennobling thoughts of God—are so alien to the natural mind; but such *is* the fact; and, according to the initiative, representative men of the present day, our fathers made a great mistake in giving so much prominence to them. The sanctified intellect of the past is with them a very common, strange, eccentric thing; and could the glorified Church once more robe herself in the garments of frailty, and come into this world again on a pilgrimage in quest of the truth, she would have to sit at the feet of some modern divines who have had little time for self-communion, and less inclination to pray; who have derived their inspiration from the pages of Carlyle or the rhapsodies of Emerson; whose especial vocation and mission appears to be to sneer at the orthodox, to sympathise with error, and to transform its egotistical progeny into something transcendent; and without shame constantly, directly or indirectly, to libel and misrepresent better men than themselves.

The *manner*, too, in which God would have His truth brought before men, is frequently very offensive to them. They love to have it introduced with a long apologetic preamble, and many polite excuses; as a trembling culprit it must ever stand at the bar of their reason; and hence, where there are not the strong convictions arising out of spiritual life, the temptation not only to bring forth but little truth, but even to present that little in such a form as to rob it of all its influence upon the conscience, frequently prevails. But can it be right to treat man with such great consideration, and God with so little—to bring God's thoughts before those whose minds are full of pride and enmity, who seldom read His Word and never pray, as so many coins which they are to chink upon the counter of depraved reason, lame logic, bald statements, crude notions, worldly systems, and idle speculations, before they admit their value or receive them, assuming that the carnal mind as such is competent to pronounce *at once* a righteous verdict upon the decisions of the great Eternal? The Apostle would not speak thus, but sought the prayers of his brethren that he might speak *boldly* as he ought to speak; and those who declare what they have tasted and handled of the Word of God, will never thus compliment the creature at the expense of the Creator. But let not the people of God be deceived; those who speak thus as they ought to speak, will ever be exposed to the educated scorn of the ignorant, and the malice of the would-be Christian leaders of transcendent doubters, whose sorrows and aspirations do *not* terminate in Christ or His exaltation, but in an ethical apotheosis of themselves, their marvellous intuitions and theological vagaries, or a Byronic dirge over their own inevitable misfortunes, but which leaves them still the slaves of sin in some form or other, but especially in bondage to the world and intellectual pride.

From the language of the Apostle, then, we may infer that there are certain truths in the revealed will of God to which the natural mind is much opposed; and that on this account there is a temptation presented to those who are engaged in its proclamation to keep them back, and that in some cases such is the actual result. Sometimes this arises from the fact that those whose duty it is to make known the truth, have never received it themselves; they have taken to the ministry as the physician takes to medicine, or the solicitor to the laws, imply for a living. These, of course, are concerned only for peace, ease, and respectability. Ministers ought to be raised above hardship and privation—of course they should; but to engage in the service of Christ, under the influence of such motives and such anticipations, never to have asked soberly and prayerfully, whether for the sake of truth and fidelity to Christ all could be sacrificed, and the path marked out by the Apostle (2 Cor. vi. 4—10) accepted, marks the character of the hireling, and not the man of God.

Some think that certain truths should be suppressed for the sake of union, as though God would have even this built upon the demoralisation of His servants.

Others imagine they shall be more useful by keeping back some of God's thoughts, though the

Apostles ever sought to lay hold of their hearers by the *whole* of God's counsel, and Christ declared, "Ye shall know the truth, and the truth shall make you free."

Some imagine they think deeply, and have more faith in their own thoughts than God's declarations. Truth is a strain of music: certain doctrines are discordant; they must never be heard. But God has written the notes; you are simply to play them, leaving the harmony or discord with him. Perhaps the music is to be heard at a greater *distance* than you imagine; or, perhaps, your ear is not quite in tune; would it not, at least, be safer to mistrust it than the notes? Years ago, through the bad results attending· an over-statement of certain doctrines, and the almost total abnegation of others, it was thought that the collective wisdom of the Fathers could be improved; the metaphysical screw was applied to certain doctrines to squeeze them into such a form as that other truths might have a more fraternal juxtaposition with them in the mind of certain persons, and that· certain dangerous symptoms affecting the body of Christ might be removed. The motive was good —doubtless there *were* things to be deplored—but the process was dangerous. The minds who applied the screw were spiritual, matured, and vigorous; others have since found it more convenient to leave those same obstreperous truths altogether. What, indeed, was wanted then, is the want now,

25*

the *old* theology—more faith in God's thoughts than man's interpretation. The church robbed of her food, or partially fed, must lose her strength. The whole truth must be preached, not as an experiment, but in faith and from a heartfelt knowledge of its power; not dealt out in infinitesimal doses as a dangerous thing from God, requiring to be corrected by our wisdom, but as the bread of the soul. Semi-converted men, by vapid declamations, intellectual platitudes, the convolutions of the imagination and flowers of rhetoric, and even by railing at and misrepresenting certain doctrines, may gather crowds to follow them who will not follow Christ nor receive his words. But to gather a different people, and produce a different result, the whole Gospel must live in the affections, as the blood dwells in the heart, and well forth from the lip as a living stream. The truth thus preached will be carried by the Holy Spirit into the heart; and like as the sap of a living tree flows into the branches to cover it with leaves and fruit, so will it appear in the life, and a spiritual, vigorous character will be formed, which, rock-like, will oppose itself to the torrents of error, pride, and worldliness, which ever spread themselves around the feet of the heaven-bound pilgrim. If there is not enough truth, however, in the ministry to form and sustain such a character, it is useless for us to complain, or to endeavour, by mere practical talk, to produce a re-

vival. The fault is with ourselves. Let us seek
to "comprehend with all saints what is the
breadth, and length, and depth, and height, and
to know the love of Christ which passeth knowledge;" and having drunk of this stream, let us
carry the living waters to others, and beneath the
blessing of God's Spirit, the waste places will soon
be made glad, and the wilderness rejoice and
blossom as the rose.

Love of popularity may in some cases lead to
the keeping back of certain doctrines, or to the
mind's dancing over the surface of truth, like the
heathen goddess, whose feet were so light that she
could pass over a field of standing corn without
shaking out a single grain—and this love of
popularity impeaches different truths in different
places. Where the people have been well fami-
liarised with the doctrines of Divine sovereignty,
electing love and particular redemption, there can
be but little temptation to keep *them* back—but
there are others equally plainly revealed; are
these proclaimed? He who said, "No man can
come unto Me except the Father who sent Me
draw him," said also, "Ye *will* not come unto Me
that ye might have life," and cried, "Repent and
believe the Gospel"—are these and other kindred
declarations heard? In other places they are
constantly iterated, but what has become of the
doctrines? On both sides, therefore, the temptation to keep back part of the truth exists, and

love of popularity on both sides may prevail to
the accomplishment of this sad result. Let not,
therefore, the hearer judge of the extent to which
it prevails by his own opinions merely, but by
the unerring Word of God. The language of
the Apostle simply points us to a fact that,
under certain circumstances, some may shun to
declare the whole counsel of God; so that it
becomes the spiritually matured, at least, to be
watchful that they are not cheated out of the
Bread of heaven, either by ignorance or want of
fidelity in those who preach the Gospel.

We must pass on, however, to notice the RE-
SULT of this keeping back of the truth, which is
fearful indeed, and such as no words can ade-
quately describe. The Apostle could say that
he was pure from the blood of all men, for that
he had not shunned to declare all the counsel of
God; the inference is, that had he not done so he
would have been guilty of their blood; and,
observe, not by the proclamation of positive
error, but by keeping back part of the truth, by
not declaring it. An awful negative is this; this,
I suppose, will be admitted, *is* "Negative Theology." Well, it has done many things—wonders, no doubt—and it will do more. It has set
up Christian men as a target for doubting, intellectual sharp-shooters, who have just sense enough
to know how to wound but not to understand
them. It has prepared many to sympathise with

and receive anything, rather than the humbling doctrines of the Cross. It has imparted to shallow, superficial thinkers an opinion that they are mental giants; and that they have a mission, and which appears to be to affect great magnanimity, humility, wonderful conflicts, and transcendent spirituality; to retail out the subtle poison of misrepresentation; to point the finger of scorn at the venerable temple of truth, and lead, helter-skelter, all who have achieved a doubt—their darling children—to a religious mirage of fantastic forms and gorgeous tints, and sparkling waters flowing above the dry and barren sands of speculation, spiritual unitarianism, and incipient infidelity; and it is to please such men that we are to shape our words! Truly, Negative Theology has done something, but there are some things it cannot do. It cannot make a Christian, nor feed him when made; but it can do something—yes; it can damn the soul! So thought, believed, and wrote the Apostle, and solemnly appealed to heaven that he was not thus guilty.

" *Pure from the blood of souls.*" It is an awful thing to have the blood of the body upon us, but a much heavier burden to have the destruction of souls upon us. Could we have witnessed the murderous Sepoys as they came forth fresh from the slaughter of our fellow-countrywomen, stained with the purple tide of their life, with what abhorrence we should have gazed upon them. With how much greater abhorrence must God look upon the man through whose want of fidelity to the truth, souls are cast into hell. A soul *lost!* What can we say, when we think of the value which God Himself has put upon it—of its vast powers and capabilities? To think that it *may* be and has been lost through want of ministerial fidelity, may well make us cry mightily to God to make and keep us faithful. Well might the Apostle exclaim, " Woe is me if I preach not the Gospel! " But, reader, there is another inference having reference to you. If you hear the Gospel fully preached, and perish, the result is not through the preacher; and as it cannot be from God, it must be therefore owing to YOURSELF! Your blood must be upon your own head. Oh, think of this, pray over it: what shall it profit you though you gain the whole world and lose your own soul?

The subject admonishes us :—

1. *To take heed* HOW *we hear.*—" Take heed how ye hear," said Christ, and that again and again; our hearing has to do not only with our present but our eternal destiny. Oh, with what humility, prayer, reverence, and dependence upon God's Spirit should we listen to the Gospel of Christ!

2. *To take heed* WHOM *we hear.*—All men have not faith, and it is certain that all men have not the truth; and even good men may for a time

yield to temptation; the fear of man may so smite them with spiritual paralysis, that the arrow of truth shall be kept at their side or fall power- less from their hands. If, therefore, we would not waste our time or lose our souls, we must take heed *who* we hear. This world's gentleman sometimes overcomes the man of God. The con- ventionalisms of respectable life rob his sword of its edge—love of praise makes it a beautiful sheath, while a fussy politeness takes the place of manly, faithful, disinterested love.

3. *To seek to know the whole truth.*—This will not ensure our spirituality *of itself,* but there can be no great spirituality without it. The blood requires all the elements of which the air is com- posed to effect its purification, and so the soul requires all the doctrines of the Gospel — the whole truth, in order to its spiritual health and sanctification. In the hands of the Spirit it is the vital sap of its strength and purity. "Sanc- tify them through thy truth, thy word is truth," said the dying Redeemer. We cannot enlarge, but ponder and pray over—Eph. iii. 17, 18, 19; Heb. vi. 1, and v. 12; Phil. i. 9, 10, 11.

4. *To receive the whole truth.*—To know it sim- ply will not save or sanctify. The poison of sin is in us; the truth must be in us too. This must be our constant and abiding concern. When, therefore, we hear that which is new to us, or, as we imagine, opposed to other doctrines, let us be

cautious lest pride, prejudice, or interest should lead us to reject any part of the counsel of God against ourselves—lest we ignorantly quarrel with a friend who is anxious simply to bless us, or reject the waters of life because they flow through channels which we approve not.

5. *To communicate the whole truth.*—There is not so much of truth in the world that we can be excused in keeping back a part. Responsibility is not confined to the pulpit in this matter: "*Ye* are my witnesses, saith the Lord." We are not to trust to ministers to do this work exclusively, nor yet to deacons, for these sometimes become so corrupted by public life and carnal policy, that they care but little for the *whole* counsel of God, and think *more* of what will bring worldly prestige and prosperity. Such do not look at man as man simply, nor truth as truth. The people must do part of the work themselves, or God will hold them responsible for it. It is not to seats of learning, to learned men or preachers, that we must look for the preservation of the truth, but to *all* who have felt and proved its *power*, the people of God in general—and hence all believers are exhorted "to contend *earnestly* for the faith once delivered to the saints." To "buy the truth and sell it not"—to be willing to part with anything to get the truth, and when it is once possessed we are never to part with it. "Take fast hold of instruction, keep her, for she

is thy life." Let us mark well the Apostle's teaching, that the church's danger does not so much arise from positive error as from the Popish doctrine of RESERVE. Let us remember that Truth is as much a stranger in the earth as ever she was, and that there are as many temptations to be faithless to her claims as ever; that, like her Lord, she often wanders here in poverty and nakedness, frequently misunderstood, misrepresented, and despised. Oh happy he who loves her at all times, and is not ashamed to stand identified with her! his path may be rough, but his end shall be peace. Are you ashamed, reader, of Truth in her robes of sorrow and humiliation? Thou shalt never see her in her exaltation in the fair palace of her Lord; for thus saith the Saviour —"Whosoever shall be ashamed of Me and of *my word*, in this adulterous and sinful generation, of him also shall the Son of Man be ashamed when He cometh in the glory of His Father with the holy angels."

"O God of truth, whose living word
Upholds whate'er had breath,
Look down on Thy creation, Lord,
Enslaved by sin and death.

Set up Thy standard, Lord, that we,
That claim a heavenly birth,
May march with Thee to smite the lies
That vex Thy groaning earth.

26

Mount Thy white horse, thou Word of God,
　Thy blood-stained vesture don:
To the last strife with death and hell
　Lead Thy great army on.

Ah! would we join that blest array,
　And follow, in the might
Of Him, the Faithful and the True,
　In raiment clean and white.

We fight for Truth, we fight for God,
　Poor slaves of liês and sin;
He who would fight for Thee on earth
　Must first be *true* within.

Then, God of Truth, for whom we long,
　Thou who wilt hear our prayer,
Do Thine own battle in our hearts,
　And slay the falsehood there.

Thou sword which goeth from His mouth,
　Smite these false hearts in twain;
Here burn, thou never-dying fire,
　Fall on, thou fiery rain!

Still smite! still burn! till nought is left
　But God's own truth and love;
Then, Lord, as morning dew comes down,
　Rest on us from above.

Yea, come! then, tried as in the fire,
　From every lie set free,
Thy perfect truth shall dwell in us,
　And we shall live in Thee."

T. HUGHES, ESQ.,
"*Lays of the Sanctuary.*"

"Oh to be
Dauntless, devoted in the war of Life—
Neither to sorrow, pain, nor trouble down
Bending thy colours, but march right through all,
Obedient to the voice that says, 'Go on!'
Oh, there are shot and shell that rend the heart,
And swords that pierce the soul, and pangs to which
A bayonet-thrust were mercy—wounds within,
That perchance bleed not in the sight of men—
Yet ah! that will not heal.   Oh, to be strong!
And with a faith enduring all things, still
To look to Thee, and battle stoutly through,
Ne'er growing weary of the glorious strife!"

" It is not strength of body, natural courage, liberal education,
bright parts, or sparkling genius, that can make a truly great
man.   Hence this seeming contradiction, yet sterling truth, *great
men are not always great.*"—*Solitude Sweetened.*

A Right Motibe;

OR,

A SUBLIME LIFE.

" For me to live is Christ."—Phil. i. 21.

THE religion of the Apostle Paul was not an accident of an accident; nor a something extrinsic
to himself—it was not like a little dust upon his
exterior, to be brushed away occasionally by accident or design; a thing to be removed by the
smallest amount of friction if rightly applied; he
did not carry it about like his clothes, and think
it quite right to cast it aside now and then, as
might best suit his purpose—no; his religion
appears thoroughly to have embraced him as well
as he it; it dwelt in him as the air in his lungs,
and the blood in his body, so that his enemies
found that, if his religion was to be got rid of, they
must get rid of *him:* Now, many would consider
this very inconvenient; and yet, having less religion than this, all real Christians would admit

26*

that we have just none at all. Now, there has
been a good deal of disputation among many about
the objective and subjective aspect of religion;
but, according to the Apostle, we certainly must
all of us be subjective enough to know that unless
the motive, power, and spring of all our efforts be
the honour of Christ, our religion is of little worth,
through whatever mediums exhibited, or however
highly esteemed by men. "For me to live is
Christ," said the Apostle—brief but emphatic
words; but embodying one of the highest mysteries of heaven, and a stretch of God's love which
can never be fully apprehended by men. The
great and good of every age have given occasional
utterance to sentiments illustrious and sublime;
but when properly understood the Apostle's words
give birth to one which in moral force and grandeur surpasses them all;—"For me to live is
Christ." This was the pole star of his faith and
life. Philosophy never dreamt of this; all truth
brought into one person to be unfolded and exhibited by myriads: and Christ is not more exalted
above men in general than was the motive of His
servant to those by which mankind for the most
part are actuated. These words, therefore, of the
Apostle *ought* to be interesting to all Christians,
for his life was undoubtedly an illustrious life,
pregnant with high and holy teaching, transcendent purity, imperishable principles, and a spiritual
influence and glory which can never die. Like

the life of its great Archetype, it passed on through
the waste places of the universe, like a beneficent
river carrying life and fruitfulness wherever it
came. Surely the source of such a life should
command our attention—"For me to live is
Christ;" here is the all-absorbing centre of my
being, around which all my thoughts, feelings,
and efforts revolve. For Christ to be *seen* is for
Him to be glorified, and hence the entire aim of
my life is the exhibition of the Son of God!
Oh! illustrious aim, sublime man! let us endeavour to ascertain, in some few particulars, how he
sought to accomplish this great result.

I. In Spirit, by the Graces he exemplified.

1. *Simple child-like faith, or habitual reliance
upon God.*—Man, as made by God, was *upright*,
fully equal to all the requirements of the law
under which he was made, while yet he was dependent upon God, both physically and morally.
Of this Adam was conscious, his experience as an
unfallen being was in accordance with the *facts*
of his existence; hence he walked as seeing "Him
who is invisible," and habitually acknowledged
God and reclined upon Him. And this, so far
from being a burden to our first parent, was a
source of joy and delight to him. Now, this was
the great central power of the moral forces within
Him, holding them together in coherence and
harmony, the result of which was peace—the *con-*

servative life of the spiritual system, the absence
of which entails ruin. Sin, however, carried man
away from God, and thus robbed him of his
strength; under its influence, too, from trusting
in God he came to trust *in himself*. And hence
his misery, weakness, timidity, and bondage to
numberless fears, which make him the slave of
circumstances and fritter away his life in inquie-
tude and unrest. To this life of *self-trust* and
worship, however, he is so wedded that the hand
of God only can separate him from it; and hence
one object which our Saviour sought to accomplish by His life and teaching was to show man
that so far from happiness being incompatible
with a life of dependence upon God, that such a
dependence was essential to its very existence,
and that if he would have rest in himself he must
have it *in God*. Hence Christ appeared below
as a poor man, and lived a life of faith upon His
Father as truly as the feeblest of His children.
And this faith of the Great Teacher we behold
reproduced by the Spirit of God in the Apostle
of the Gentiles: we find him constantly acknow-
ledging his God and Father, and glorying in his
weakness, "that the power of God may rest upon
him."

2. *Profound reverence for the Word of God.*—
Our Saviour perpetually referred to the Word of
God as His text-book, guide, and directory: "I
came," He says, "not to do my own will, but the

will of Him that sent me." And the same spirit lived in the Apostle who perpetually supported the doctrines he taught by the Word of God. (Acts xiii. 17.)

3. *Disinterested love and self-sacrifice.*—The burden of the law was "thou shalt love the Lord thy God with all thy heart, and with all thy soul, and with all thy mind, and thy neighbour as thyself." And how beautifully do we see this precept exemplified in the life of Christ; and the Apostle was no dreamy sentimentalist, talking and writing pretty things about self-sacrifice, overlooking the great sacrifice of the Son of God; but while laying this as the only basis of a sinner's hope, his life was one scene of the purest love, and anxious toil, and disinterested labour for the salvation of men. How repeatedly did he affirm that he was willing to die for the sake of the Gospel and people of God; "I endure all things," says he, "for the elect's sake, that they may also obtain the salvation which is in Christ Jesus with eternal glory."

4. *Faithfulness.*—The world, sometimes, has much to say about faithfulness; but we must not forget that Christ was the faithful and true witness, in a certain sense the only one the world ever saw, and yet it crucified Him. God, to put men to the test and manifest their spirit, brought all truth into one living page, and presented it for perusal, and they put their hands upon it at once,

and tore it to pieces. Our Saviour, we are told, "was faithful in all His house," and the great Apostle had His spirit; "moreover," says he, "it is required of stewards that a man be found faithful." He saw that he was in the midst of an *unreal* world, and that men were taken up with shams and loved smooth things; that a religion of *power* would have no friends but those whom God made, and that truth was liable to be killed by the courtesies of life, and that it was possible for the spirit of this world to overcome the man of God. And hence he aimed to be faithful; it was the very height of his ambition as a good soldier of Jesus Christ; not that he indulged in practical talk without a conscience, rattling away under the influence of a professional habit, thinking that this was the object to be desiderated. He did not fling the precepts of Christ at men as so many stones, under the influence of a heathenish spirit; nor did he find it *easy* to preach them, while he remembered that he *ought* also to practise them: and hence in his most faithful utterances he identified himself with the people to whom he addressed himself in all their sorrows and conflicts, and as standing in need of the same corrective words which he administered to others. Nor did the Apostle aim to be faithful by perpetually finding fault with everybody and everything, for he loved to commend what was good. But he was true to the light that was in him; and the truth which

Christ had taught and made precious in his experience he freely proclaimed, whether men would hear or forbear. A proud, haughty, overbearing spirit he never manifested, nor put on an affected dignity on account either of his great knowledge or public services; he was really *great* because unconscious of his greatness; and so truly humble that the feeblest babe in grace would approach him with confidence as *a brother*. All his spiritual power and beauty arose out of what *he was*, and sprang forth from his new nature like the blossoms and fruit of a living tree. He was a powerful reasoner, not by the aid of formal logic, but a holy life, and the truth he preached he sublimely knew, because he lived it. His whole life constrained him to tell the whole truth, and hence he was often most faithful when least he knew it; while yet, knowing the sensibilities of spiritual life, he knew also how to sustain it beneath the dissecting knife of truth. The faithfulness of the Apostle, however, was not a noisy, impudent, and obtrusive thing; it was not like the thunder-storm, but the gently-descending rain which melts the unsightly clods and makes them fruitful; his knife *was* keen, and hence it passed into the conscience without a great noise. He was faithful to his principles, nor less with persons; he courted not the smile of the great, nor feared the frowns of the ignorant. Though prepared to render honour to whom honour was due, in his public capacity as a preacher of the Gospel he dealt with men as men, and permitted not their predilections nor prejudices, nor the conventionalisms of life to rob his sword of its edge. He thought more of God than men ; of truth more than human opinions.

5. *Tenderness.*—Of our exalted Redeemer it was written, " He shall not break the bruised reed, nor quench the smoking flax." With the incorruptible fidelity of the faithful and true witness, He combined the most inimitable tenderness; and most ardently did the Apostle Paul emulate His spirit. However searching and corrective the words of this great man fall upon the Christian's ear, he ever feels that it is a loving brother who is dealing with his conscience. This world is faithless and cruel; it is capable of judgment, but not mercy : men, being aliens from God, are aliens from each other, and frequently, in their self-righteous and ignorant zeal, would not only correct but destroy each other. The Apostle is altogether free from this spirit; he wounded but to heal, and the two-edged sword of the Spirit was ever wielded by him with the greatest tenderness and love. And surely, amid the artificialities, flatteries, falsehoods, and frequently cruelty of both the Church and the world, every Christian should aim to embody in his life and conduct the tenderness of that Apostle who in all things could say, " for me to live is

Christ;" and to labour like him to be *sincere,* amid an atmosphere of insincerity; to struggle to be *real* while thousands are perpetually seeking to hide themselves behind the mask of false appearances!

II. IN WORD, BY THE DOCTRINES HE PROCLAIMED. " We preach not ourselves," said he, " but Christ Jesus the Lord;" and in another place, " I determined not to know anything among you, save Jesus Christ, and Him crucified;" and, writing to the Galatians, he exclaims; " But God forbid that I should glory, save in the Cross of our Lord Jesus Christ, by whom the world is crucified unto me, and I unto the world." This celebrated apostle would have Christ incarnated by God's Spirit in all his thoughts, and in every truth he proclaimed; he was a graphic spiritual artist, and his preaching was a picture in which Christ crucified was ever the centre object. And the Apostle took this course, not from ignorance nor narrowness of mind, but from knowledge and a comprehensive view of the will of God, and of both sanctified and unsanctified nature. He knew, from the promises of God and his own experience, that Christ must be the sun of his doctrinal system, if its several truths were to be clothed with spiritual beauty, and made attractive to the faith of real Christians, or to exert a vivifying and fertilizing influence upon the hearts of men in general; hence, how-

27

ever' broken, incoherent, and unsystematized his writings or utterances may seem to be, the spiritual eye will ever perceive that he placed Christ in the centre as a magnet to bring them together, to vitalize them, and give them unity and force upon the conscience. The Gospel in his hands, like a kaleidoscope, constantly presented truths in various forms and colours, the whole of which, however, through the light of God's Spirit, perpetually blended together to form but one image, the consummate beauty and instructive perfection of which eternity will never fully reveal—that of Him who, in the estimation of every saint, is "the chief among ten thousand, and the altogether lovely;" a man of sorrows, it is true, with a head crowned with thorns, a body broken and pierced with nails, but a centre of profound mystery, divine wisdom, and moral utterance, upon which the highest intelligences of heaven gaze with holy reverence, wonder, and delight—a page of truth comprehending and embracing all other truths, and bringing each divergent line of this world's mysteries and sorrows into the all-absorbing infinite and inimitable centre of Jehovah's LOVE. This, the key-stone of that arch which spans the Divine perfections, the basis of those attributes which form the very nature of God— which, *in union with His justice*, becomes the great healer of all man's grief, the foundation of his undying bliss and everlasting triumph over sin,

death, and hell—throws forth its brightness and
beauty through the Cross of Christ; and hence
all the words of this well-instructed scribe and
illustrious apostle, went but to form the god-like
base and column of his public work, upon the
golden apex of which in characters of light were
ever inscribed the one great legend of this world's
sins and sorrows, and the great remedy of all its
woes—" CHRIST CRUCIFIED."

III. DEEDS.—The life of the Apostle Paul was
not only sublime in words, but WORK. He not
only spoke well, but he did well: his actions
gave emphasis to his teaching; he could say,
"These things which ye have both learned and
received, and heard and *seen* in me, do, and the
God of heaven shall be with you;" and it is this
union of right principles with right conduct
which constitutes a great life. And as Christ
was the centre of all the Apostle's words, so he
was no less the life of all his deeds; hence, as his
words had a noble meaning, so had also his actions, and both terminated in one object, the
exaltation of the Son of God. The Apostle's life,
therefore, was, in the highest sense, a great *speaking* life—full of holy and instructive lessons,
copied from the life of the Great Exemplar. The
activities of his bodily and mental powers were
not the movements of a mere intellectual machine,
on which little meaning and no moral aim could
be written, but they were the visible embodiments

of a holy and spiritual intelligence in him, as truly related to Christ as the needle to the pole. The biography of the Apostle, therefore, was great, because filled with a greater than himself; and so far from his words and deeds resembling those of a mere automaton, or intended by him to accomplish but another incarnation of himself before the eye of his mind or the gaze of the world, they were charged with a more exalted mission, and designed by him to issue in a constant apocalypse of His Lord and Master. And thus the fame which others seek to obtain by labouring to exalt themselves, he unconsciously achieved by living to make known another; the entire hemisphere of his receptive and active life being filled with Christ, his words and deeds are as imperishable as the life from whence they sprang, and from them springs forth an influence, the waves of which not only rise and spread over the ocean of time, but break forth in one ceaseless, everlasting anthem upon the shores of eternity.

O reader! what dost thou know of this vital, soul-transforming Christianity, of which Christ is the centre and circumference? Dost thou aim to exhibit Him in spirit, word, and deed? The priests of Rome tell us that even right principles are too abstract, and that we fail in our Christianity because we have not a priest to embody and give them a practical exemplification before us; but, oh, we fail, not because we have not a priest, for we have One of whom it is witnessed that "HE EVER LIVETH," but because we seek not that grace which lived in the heart of the Apostle of the Gentiles, and which made his life so beautiful a transcript of heaven's richest mercy, wisdom, and love. Alas! what poor artists we are at best, and how frequently our most elaborate attempts to portray the "Fairest of the Fair" do but hide His beauty. May we at least have the humility which becomes the initial lines of the great Picture we have dared to set before us, and, above all, be kept from an affected magnanimity which more than anything transforms us into so many caricatures of Him who was meek and lowly in heart.

But it may be profitable for us before we close this paper to notice what is involved in the development and maintenance of this life, and some of its advantages.

THE DEVELOPMENT AND MAINTENANCE OF THIS LIFE. Many things are involved:—

1. *Spiritual Life.*—As all the external beauty and fruit of a tree springs from the living sap of the root, so all the spiritual and practical beauty of the Christian must spring from a principle of spiritual life ever in connexion with its great Author, or it will perish; as our Saviour admonished us when, speaking of certain hearers of the Gospel, He said, "and because they had no root in themselves they withered away."

27*

2. *Dependence.*—"We are not sufficient of our-selves to think a good thought as of ourselves," said the Apostle, "but our sufficiency is of God." "Abide in me," said Christ, "and I in you; as the branch cannot bear fruit of itself except it abide in the vine, no more can ye except ye abide in me." If we .are to bear the fruit, there-fore, of the TRUE VINE, we must receive of its living sap, and look to Christ constantly for the renewings of His Divine Spirit.

3. *Watchfulness.*—How carefully does the artist watch his hand when imparting to his picture those minute touches upon the precision of which the life and beauty of his picture depends; and how watchful must the Christian be over his *little* words, tempers and things, if he would have it known and felt that "for him to live is Christ."

4. *Diligence.*—It has been said of one of the pictures of a certain artist, that every square inch of its surface, when brought under the glass, exhi-bits marks of genius, and the closest study and observation of Nature in all her changing moods and manifestations; and oh, if our life in the remotest degree, is to be a transcript of *One* who was the perfection of beauty, what labour we must expend upon it! And if men, in the pursuit of a passing glory, will expend so much toil upon a piece of canvas to exhibit but a passing gleam of this world's glory, how much more labour should we willingly devote to the perfection of a spirit

which can receive and exhibit an imperishable beauty before the throne of God!

5. *Prayer.*—He who would exhibit Christ must walk with Christ; it is by communion with Him that we catch His Spirit. Prayer keeps us from fainting beneath the imperfection of our own efforts, revives the drooping heart, and gives tranquillity and strength to the mind, to sketch in, upon the crossed and blotted page of life, some at least of the heavenly lineaments of Divine pity, purity, mercy and love, so that all is not quite confusion and darkness. Oh, ye prayerless souls, what a dark enigma must your lives be, both to yourselves and others! Know ye that the elements of a great character are developed and matured by divine Mercy, and that she stoops only to embrace her children upon the knee of prayer, and beneath the golden propitiatory of a Saviour's righteousness.

THE ADVANTAGES OF THIS LIFE :—

1. *It will give a dignity and grandeur to our existence.*—An exalted aim will impart greatness to any man's life, however humble or insignificant he may be in the estimation of the world. And what is the aim of a real Christian? to exhibit Christ, to embody His teachings in his life, and to exemplify His graces. It is while daring to make this attempt, that he learns what Christ *is ;* and while he thus realizes his own littleness and insufficiency, his feeblest efforts raise him to a

moral and spiritual elevation he never otherwise
would have perceived or known. Actuated by
such a motive, the whole of the Christian's life
becomes sublime, pregnant with Divine principles
and undying thoughts. The smallest affairs of
life, as we deem them, gather a meaning from the
purpose to which they are subordinated, and
assume a shape and beauty, in the eyes even of
the Great Eternal, and in relation to the Divine
object, which, like the minute touches of the
artist's pencil, they are intended to portray.

2. *An intelligent unity to life.*—What a number
of valuable lives are lost, for want of unity of
moral aim! Now it is thought this is of import
ance, and now that. Now it is a moral apho-
rism, now a law of etiquette, now a piece of
ritualism; many things in turn and nothing
long. Oh, how many, at the close of life, behold
all their efforts lie together, a rude and senseless
heap, without form, coherence, or meaning; upon
which, in their dying hour, they write vanity and
vexation of spirit, and depart, having exerted no
permanent, elevating influence over their fellow-
creatures. The Christian escapes this: the one
object for which he lives, in the hands of God's
Spirit, gives a force and vitality to his labours, so
that he cannot live in vain; wherever he goes, he
has a clear perception of *his work*, and of the great
business of life; nor does he waste his time looking after either his implements or companions.

In reference to the former, the words of Jesus and the hand of faith are all he needs; while, as it regards the latter, those who serve his Lord best are his selected friends. Thus he is neither driven nor drifted by the strong current of life into either his creed or connexions, but selects both under the guidance of the life which is in him, and with a view to the great object to which, constrained by Divine love, he has consecrated all his powers.

3. *Perpetuity.*—Of the Christian, it is written " He shall grow as the lily, and cast forth his roots as Lebanon. His branches shall spread, and his beauty shall be as the olive tree, and his smell as Lebanon. They that dwell under his shadow shall return; they shall revive as the corn, and grow as the vine: the scent thereof shall be as the wine of Lebanon." In constantly returning to God in Christ, the believer exerts an influence upon himself and others which shall never die; and the fair outlines of truth which he is instrumental in stamping upon the heart in the exhibition of Christ, shall never be effaced; while the pure current of that happiness which he finds in his aim and work, shall continue to rise and rise, until it reaches the throne of God and the Lamb, where, spreading like a sea of glass, it shall for ever reflect, in all their perfection and beauty, the spiritual lineaments of Him, whose grace, rich, free, and abundant, bade it to gush forth in the heart and life of an alien and stranger.

In conclusion, dear reader, how different is the life of a real Christian from that of a mere ritualist, or man of the world! The former lives to exhibit Christ; the latter himself, or some part or parts of a dead material system. We perceive what the Christian cannot be—he cannot be an egotist, for he lives to exhibit another: we see what he *must* be, an epistle of Christ. The true believer would have his entire life built up as a chaste temple to the memory of Jesus. What the Christian is to be in heaven he desires to be here, a mirror in the hand of Love, perpetually reflecting the beauty of his Lord. How worthless is profession without Christ! how vain our anticipation of heaven! Without Christ we can only exhibit Satan and ourselves;—this may be allowed in this world, but not in that which is to come. ' Real greatness, then, does not consist in mere intellectual power, wealth, or skill in things human or divine; but in the conformity of our minds to Christ. And this greatness is accessible to the poor as well as the rich, the learned and the unlearned—a greatness upon which even God will smile, which emulates and embodies the perfections of His Son, and derives an imperishable beauty, fragrance, and beneficence from the constant ministrations and discipline of the Eternal Spirit; and which, when all the greatness of this world, with all its manifold signs and symbols, shall have passed away, robed in the righteousness of Christ, shall lift its regal head among the sons of God, and even there, in other forms and more illustrious words, shall still give utterance to the glorious theme, "FOR ME TO LIVE IS CHRIST." May the Apostle's prayer, therefore, be ours:—"THAT I MAY KNOW HIM, AND THE POWER OF HIS RESURRECTION, AND THE FELLOWSHIP OF HIS SUFFERINGS, BEING MADE CONFORMABLE UNTO HIS DEATH!"

"NOW UNTO HIM THAT IS ABLE TO KEEP YOU FROM FALLING, AND TO PRESENT YOU FAULT-LESS BEFORE THE PRESENCE OF HIS GLORY WITH EXCEEDING JOY,

"TO THE ONLY WISE GOD, OUR SAVIOUR, BE GLORY AND MAJESTY, DOMINION AND POWER, BOTH NOW AND EVER. AMEN."

"My Father! Heavenly Father! to whom sole
I lift my eye in trouble or in joy,—
Thou who hast led me, erst a wayward child,—
And wayward still, from weakness, not from choice,—
And brought me thus far on my journey's way,
Grant in the years to come I still may prove
Obedient to the imperial Voice within ;
Voice of that soul which Thou hast given ; which bids
Still to go forward, resting not till death.
Oh! make me strong, that so when sorrows come,
When loved ones die and leave me, and the day
Grows dark about me, and the sunshine comes
To the heart no more, and the Spirit's life seems gone
With the love that fed it, I may still march on,
Content to do Thy work, and heed no more
Whether the clarion-voice of fame do come
In life, or after death, or not at all.

Oh, be it mine, at life's bless'd close, to stand,
Scarr'd though it be with sorrows, still erect,
In harness to the last,—raising my hands
On the won battle-field aloft to Thee,
And with a calm joy yielding up my soul,—
Scourged. chastened, purified,—and hearing now
The inner voices chanting victory!
Like some old warrior-chief, on his last field,
Dying with upturned face, and in his ears
An army's songs of triumph;—heedless all,
If so be the stern fight is won at last,
And his flag flies, victorious still in death."

THE END.

THE BAPTIST CHURCH DIRECTORY:

A Guide to the Doctrines, Discipline, Officers, Ordinances, and Customs of Baptist Churches. By EDWARD T. HISCOX, D. D. Price, red edges, 60 cents; plain, 50 cents.

"It will prove, in my judgment, an invaluable guide to our church members."—*Dr. Jeter, of Richmond.*

LIFE OF SPENCER H. CONE, D. D. With

a fine Steel Plate Portrait. 1 vol. 12mo. Price $1 25.

"A complete, accurate, and in every way reliable memoir of our lamented brother."—*New York Chronicle.*

GRACE TRUMAN; or, Love and Principle.

By SALLIE ROCHESTER FORD. With Steel Portrait of the Authoress. 1 vol. 12mo. Price $1.

PRINCIPLES AND PRACTICES OF BAP-

TISTS. By FRANCIS WAYLAND, D. D. 1 vol. 12mo. Price, $1.

THE BAPTIST DENOMINATION. By

Rev. D. C. HAYNES. With an Introduction by Rev. JOHN DOWLING, D. D. 1 vol. 12mo. Price $1.

THE BAPTIST LIBRARY. A Republica-

tion of Standard Baptist Works. Edited by Rev. Messrs. G. G. SOMERS, W. R. WILLIAMS, and L. L. HILL. 1 vol. royal octavo. Sheep. $3 50.

BENEDICT'S HISTORY OF THE BAP-

TISTS. A General History of the Baptist Denomination in America, and other parts of the World. By DAVID BENEDICT. With a Steel Portrait of Roger Williams. 1 vol. royal octavo. Sheep. Price $3 50.

COMPENDIUM OF THE FAITH OF THE

BAPTISTS. Paper. Price, per dozen, 50 cents.

BLIND BARTIMEUS; Or, The Story of a

Sightless Sinner and his Great Physician. By Rev. WILLIAM J. HOGE, Professor in the Union Theological Seminary, Prince Edwards, Va. 1 vol. large 18mo. 257 pages. 75 cents.

"A most excellent book, full of sound instruction and the very spirit of the Gospel."—*Boston Recorder.*

" We wish it could be placed, this winter, in the hands of thousands of 'sightless sinners.' "—*Cincinnati Christian Herald.*

" Brief in compass, clear in arrangement, and singularly animated, direct, forcible, and pungent in style, not rarely reminding one of the fervor of Richard Baxter, while marked throughout by a classic elegance of diction, to which he made no pretension."—*Cor. N. C. Presbyterian.*

DAILY THOUGHTS FOR A CHILD. By

Mrs. THOMAS GELDART, author of " Truth is Every Thing," " Emilie the Peacemaker," etc., etc. 1 vol. 18mo. 50 cents.

"In exquisite simplicity of style, beauty of illustration, and religious power, this book has few superiors in juvenile literature."—*Boston Era.*

"Meditations for morning and evening for a month, adapted to the capacity and aspirations of a youthful heart. Many of them are very sweet and affecting compositions."

"A charming little work, which is sure to be a favorite with the young."—*English Papers.*

TRUTH IS EVERY THING. By Mrs.

THOMAS GELDART. 1 vol. 18mo. Price 50 cents.

" The interest of the volume is genuine. There is nothing false or spurious about it. It is true to nature; it is true to the heart."

" This is a charming little book for the young; the matter is very interesting, not overdrawn, while its tenor is to win over youth to the practice and love of truth."

" This is a charming tale, attractive from the simplicity and beauty of feeling which pervades it—most useful because it steps not beyond the comprehension of youth."—*English Press.*

THE LIVING EPISTLE ; or, The Moral

Power of a Religious Life. By Rev. CORNELIUS TYREE, of Powhatan, Va. With an Introduction by Rev. Dr. FULLER, of Baltimore. 1 vol. 18mo. Price 60 cents.

"It is adapted to the wants of the times, and, we trust, will be extensively read."—*Southern Baptist Missionary Magazine.*

"A book full of good counsels, important lessons, elevating the idea of the Christian life, and encouraging the reader to holy living and action."—*New York Observer.*

SUMMER PICTURES FROM COPENHAGEN TO VENICE. By Rev. HENRY M. FIELD. 1 vol. 12mo. Price $1.

Mr. Field's book gives lively pictures of the Continent and its inhabitants, and is particularly valuable for its descriptions of northern Italy, the scene of the coming conflict. It will be a popular and very interesting volume for summer reading.

THE LOSING AND TAKING OF MANSOUL; or, Lectures on the Holy War. By Rev. A. S. PATTON, A.M. 1 vol. 12mo. Illustrated with Eight spirited Engravings. Price $1.

" He writes well and forcibly."—*Philadelphia Ledger.*

" The eminent author of this work has compressed into a brief space a comprehensive review of the evils which, without religious influences, everywhere abound in society, and the effective means with which to correct them. It is the result of a life-time of deep thought and close observation."—*Dubuque Times.*

THE "PRECIOUS STONES OF THE HEAVENLY FOUNDATIONS." By AUGUSTA BROWN GARRET. 1 vol. 18mo. Price $1.

" A book of great beauty, and full of attractive discourse on heavenly and divine things."—*New York Observer.*

" The articles are brief, and include many choice specimens of prose and poetry. It is especially adapted to lay on the center-table, or elsewhere, for the casual reader."—*Congregationalist.*

" The book is a suggestive one, and needs but a slight examination to become a favorite with the religious portion of the community."—*Boston Post.*

MEMOIR OF REV. DAVID T. STODDARD. By Rev. J. P. THOMPSON, D. D. 1 vol. 12mo. Price $1.

" A biography of serene beauty and abiding value."—*New Englander.*

" All Sabbath School libraries and all students should especially make sure of the possession of this volume."—*Congregationalist.*

" The entire volume proffers numerous claims to an extended circulation."—*North American.*

THE CHRISTIAN GRACES. By Rev. J. P.
THOMPSON, D.D., of the Broadway Tabernacle. 1 vol. 18mo Price 75 cents.

"The book is well fitted to do good to all everywhere; and we hope it will be widely read, and made greatly useful."—*New York Observer.*

"Dr. Thompson has a happy talent for the familiar exposition of Scripture, and the practical application of its doctrines."—*Boston Recorder.*

"They are earnest and affectionate exhortations, intended to help in the formation of Christian character, and the cultivation of the Christian graces."—*Boston Advertiser.*

THE BIBLE IN THE LEVANT; or, The
Life and Letters of Rev. CHESTER N. RIGHTER. By Rev. S. IRENÆUS PRIME, D.D. Illustrated with a Steel Portrait of Mr. Righter. 1 vol. 18mo. 336 pages. Price 75 cents.

"The results of his efforts are narrated by Mr. Prime in a style clear and interesting, which renders this volume not only readable, but exceedingly instructive. We can commend the work with entire confidence that it will be productive of good results."—*Boston Post.*

"It is really beautiful in its delineation of a frank, whole-souled man, who always pressed straight forward in the fear of God, without any fear of man."—*Hartford Courant.*

"Mr. Righter's visit to the Copts, in Egypt, and description of that interesting people, will be read with peculiar interest. The account of his travels is taken principally from his letters, and displays, unconsciously, his bold, fearless, unwavering devotion to the right. His biographer was his traveling companion in his first tour abroad, and enjoyed peculiar advantages for thoroughly comprehending his character."—*Boston Journal.*

GLIMPSES OF JESUS, EXALTED IN THE
AFFECTIONS OF HIS PEOPLE. By Rev. W. P BALFERN. 1 vol. 18mo. Price 60 cents.

"This book is redolent with the sweet savor of Him whose name is like precious ointment poured forth."—*Evangelical Repository.*

"Few works of this class are to be named with it, and as a Sabbath School volume it stands, we should think, almost without a rival."—*Boston Daily Traveller.*

"This is a sweet little book. Many a halting pilgrim will be quickened, many awakened ones will be led to Jesus, and many stricken souls will be revived and comforted by a perusal of its pages, beaming with a Saviour's love."—*Presbyterian Banner and Advocate.*

"It presents the example of Christ under the various circumstances and vicissitudes of his brief earthly history, for the imitation and encouragement of his followers."—*American Presbyterian and Genessee Evangelist.*